a bible study for teen girls

CONFIDENT

CAROL SALLEE

LifeWay Press®
Nashville, Tennessee

ISBN: 9781415867198
Item: 005189794

Dewey Decimal Classification: 248.83
Subheading: GIRLS \ TEENAGERS \ CONFIDENCE

Printed in the United States of America

Student Ministry Publishing
LifeWay Christian Resources
One LifeWay Plaza, MSN 144
Nashville, TN 37234-0144

We believe that the Bible has God for its author; salvation for its end; and truth, without any
mixture of error, for its matter and that all Scripture is totally true and trustworthy.
To review LifeWay's doctrinal guideline, please visit www.lifeway.com/doctrinalguideline.

All Scripture quotations are taken from the
Holman Christian Standard Bible®, copyright © 1999, 2000, 2002, 2003
by Holman Bible Publishers. Used by permission.

Contents

About the Author

Carol Sallee is a motivational speaker and freelance writer from Oklahoma. She is the founder of To Know Christ Ministries. Through this ministry, Carol speaks across the United States and writes for a variety of publications. Carol is married to Phil and is mom to Julie, Jill, and Josh.

Carol met Phil in high school at a leadership weekend for student council presidents. On her first day at the University of Tulsa, Carol discovered she had three classes with Phil. Their first date was on a Friday night to a college Valentine's Day banquet. One month later, Phil led Carol to a personal relationship with Jesus Christ. About one year later, they were married and were working together at a church. Twenty-nine years later, Carol and her husband still have a date every Friday night and continue to serve in the ministry.

Carol could go on and on about her three grown children, but thinks these descriptions give the general idea: "Julie is one of the most creative and original people I've ever known. Jill has the skills and the drive to be either the first female president of the United States or the dictator of a small country. Josh could fill a stadium with his charisma and personality."

A great evening to Carol involves a good movie and Mexican food. Her favorite quote hangs above the computer at which she does most of her writing: "The point of life's journey is not to arrive at the grave safely with a well-preserved body; but rather to skid in sideways, hair a mess, totally worn out, shouting, 'Woohoo! What a ride!'"

Carol is excited you've agreed to come along on this ride with her and hopes you'll let her know about your journey toward confidence by contacting her on Facebook or on her Web site at *www.carolsallee.com*.

Introduction

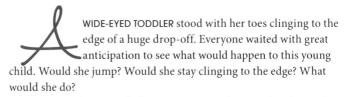

WIDE-EYED TODDLER stood with her toes clinging to the edge of a huge drop-off. Everyone waited with great anticipation to see what would happen to this young child. Would she jump? Would she stay clinging to the edge? What would she do?

OK. So maybe it wasn't that exciting. But when my daughter, Julie, was two years old, her dad decided he wanted to teach her to have complete confidence in him. To do this, he stood her up in the middle of our couch, stepped back two feet, stretched his arms out toward her, and said, "Come on, Julie! Trust!" The response he wanted from her was the response he got. She threw her arms out to the side, tilted her head toward the ceiling, shouted "Trust!," and leapt into her dad's outstretched arms. They did this over and over, and he caught her every time. To increase Julie's confidence, her dad next put her on the back of the couch, then on the top of the dryer, and then on the top of the refrigerator. Each time the scene was repeated: "Come on, Julie! Trust!"

What would inspire a toddler to leap from the top of a kitchen appliance? It was the presence of her dad. There was just something reassuring about his outstretched arms that were ready to catch her.

Fast-forward fourteen years, and this same girl was standing on the top of a cliff. Our family was at the lake with another family who had a cabin and a boat. Both families had loaded into the boat and had ridden to an area of the lake where impressive cliffs stood with deep water below them. The kids all climbed to the top of the highest cliff and were taking turns jumping into the water. The parents sat nearby in the boat watching the kids take the plunge. Every kid had splashed into the water—except Julie. She stood with her toes clinging to the edge of the cliff for thirty minutes. About every two minutes she said, "Oh! I almost went!" It didn't look to us like she moved at all.

The sun was beginning to set. We needed to get this girl off that cliff and safely into the boat. We knew it would be easier for Julie to jump into the water than to climb back down the cliff, so she was going to have to take the leap. We waited. We watched. She hedged. Suddenly, her dad hopped out of the boat and into the water and swam near where Julie would land if she finally found the confidence to jump. He stretched his arms out toward her and said, "Come on, Julie! Trust!" The response he wanted from her was the response he got. She threw her arms out, tilted her head toward the sky, shouted "Trust!," and leapt into the water near her dad.

What made the difference for Julie that day as she clung to the edge of that cliff? It was the presence of her dad. There was just something reassuring about him being nearby, ready to catch her or rescue her.

Maybe you can relate to Julie's story. Oh, you're not on a real cliff, but it sure feels that way. When you get up every day, life just feels too risky. You feel afraid and uncertain about your place in the world. Your toes are clinging to the edge, and you don't have the confidence to take the leap and live your life in the way God intended you to live it.

What will make the difference? The only thing that will truly get you off that cliff is the presence of your Father—your Heavenly Father. Abba.

The world tries to fool you into believing you can find the confidence you need in a myriad of ways. Social status. Popularity. The right clothes, the right hairstyle, and the right boyfriend. The problem with all of these things is that they are temporary. A girl can go from the "It Girl" to a social outcast in a matter of minutes. Clothing and hairstyles change overnight. Boyfriends come and go. If you build your confidence on these fleeting things, you're going to get stuck up on that cliff, with no real assurance of yourself or anything around you.

If you're struggling to really live your life to the fullest, then you've come to the right study. It's designed to help you find the confidence that only God can give. The kind of confidence that lasts a lifetime. The kind of confidence that inspires you to take risks. The kind of confidence that no one can take away from you.

It's my heart's desire that you will be changed through the study of God's Word and through the thoughts expressed on the pages of this book. This study was born out of my own lack of confidence. It came from looking around at the girls in my life and realizing that we are all plagued by a lack of confidence. In fact, it almost looks like it's an epidemic. How did this happen? Where did it come from? Is this really how God intended His daughters to live? I don't believe so.

Over the next six weeks, you'll discover a different way to live your life. You will find the real you—the one God intended when He created you.

Come on! Trust! Take the leap.
The world is waiting on you!

Original Design

"With confidence, you can reach truly amazing heights; without confidence, even the simplest accomplishments are beyond your grasp."
—Unknown

Jill won her first beauty pageant when she was in high school. She went on to win a pageant at her college and to compete at the state pageant. One of the things Jill had to prepare for each pageant was her platform. Pageant contestants are required to choose a platform—a social issue they are dedicated to and wish to promote. Jill chose abstinence and sexual purity as her platform. It was an issue in which she believed she could make a difference in the lives of teens.

In political campaigns, politicians choose platforms, too. They choose topics, principles, or issues and make them the focus of their speeches and efforts on behalf of our country. It might be abortion, protecting the environment, rights for the homeless, tort law reform, or tax breaks for a specific group of people.

If you had to choose a social platform or take a stand on an issue, what would it be? Why is this platform or issue important to you?

Much like a pageant contestant or a politician (of which I am neither!), I have a platform, too. My issue is this: the widespread lack of confidence in young women. I believe it's an issue in which God wants to make a difference in the lives of teen girls and women.

But before we can really talk about this issue, we need to stop and clarify a few things. How would you define the words "confidence" and "confident"?

Confidence is:

To be confident means:

Based on your definitions, can you remember a time in your life when you felt really confident? What was happening in your life that made you feel that way?

"If you really put a small value upon yourself, rest assured that the world will not raise your price."
—Unknown

Dictionaries define these words like this:

Confidence
Full trust or faith in the powers, trustworthiness, or reliability of a person or a thing.[1]

Confident
To have strong belief or full assurance.[2]
To be fully convinced of something.

How did your definitions differ from the dictionary's definitions?

Maybe your definitions were right on the mark, maybe not. But even the dictionary's definitions fall short. Why? There's no mention of God in either definition. Now, if you include Him in the definition, it revolutionizes the meaning. But how?

For it was You who created my inward parts; You knit me together in my mother's womb. I will praise You, because I have been remarkably and wonderfully made. Your works are wonderful, and I know this very well. My bones were not hidden from You when I was made in secret, when I was formed in the depths of the earth. Your eyes saw me when I was formless; all my days were written in Your book and planned before a single one of them began.
—Psalm 139:13-16

THE WRONG SOURCE

Confidence is full trust in God and in His abilities. It's believing He is trustworthy and reliable. Confidence is about having complete faith in Him, not in yourself. And that's a great place to put your confidence because He never fails. He is perfect. What He does prospers. But the world tries to convince you that confidence is somehow about you and what you can do (or don't do).

Think about the typical girl. On the list below, check the things that girls your age use to make themselves feel more confident.

♡ Good looks

♡ Great body

♡ Pretty smile

♡ Clear skin

♡ Cute boyfriend

♡ Stylish wardrobe

♡ Cool car

♡ Beautiful hair

♡ Cheerleader

♡ Starter on sports team

♡ Fancy house

♡ Being part of the popular crowd

♡ Member of specific club or group

♡ Dazzling personality

♡ Funny

♡ Good grades

♡ Respected family

♡ Popularity

♡ Money

♡ Other: _____

What's the problem with these sources of confidence?

_____

_____

They're all temporary. With enough time (and in some cases, no time at all) any one of these things could be taken away. None of them is permanent. A car rusts. A stylish wardrobe goes out of style. Popularity changes in an instant. Money dries up.

Go back to the list on the previous page, and beside each thing you checked, write a brief description of how each of these things is temporary. In the space below, write down the various ways each could be lost, stolen, or taken away.

_____

_____

_____

_____

It's important for you to understand that confidence should have nothing to do with your looks, your body, or random status symbols like clothes or hairstyles. Sure, everyone likes to wear a new outfit and top it off with a good hair day. But if your confidence—how you feel about yourself and your abilities—is completely wrapped up in those clothes or that hair, then you're hanging by a thread, so to speak.

At the end of the day there's a stain from lunch on your new outfit, your hair has flopped thanks to the rain, and your feet hurt in those trendy shoes. If you base your confidence on the kinds of things you checked on the list, you're done. Tomorrow morning you will have to hunt for a whole new source of confidence in your closet or in front of your mirror.

THE RIGHT SOURCE

Being a confident young woman means you are fully convinced of God's love for you. You believe what He says, not what everyone else says. God-confidence means you trust in and depend on the strength of Christ. You are completely assured He is charge of your life and wants you to become all that He designed you to be. That kind of God-confidence is designed to last a lifetime. That kind of confidence looks good on a girl—it radiates off of her.

Rate your God-confidence using the statements below.

Never

Rarely

Sometimes

Most of the Time

Always

I have faith in God and His abilities.
I believe God is trustworthy and reliable.
I am fully convinced of God's love for me.
I trust what God says in His Word.
I know God will never abandon me.
I am confident God has a plan for my life.

How did you rate? Check the statement you think best applies to you:
_____ My God-confidence level is really high.
_____ My God-confidence is good on most days, but sometimes I
wonder...
_____ I am struggling to believe God cares about me or my life.
_____ I think He goofed up somehow when He made me.

Pause for a moment to honestly reflect:
Do you feel like a confident girl? If so, on what are you basing
your confidence? If not, what's keeping you from living with the
confidence God intended?

EPIDEMIC OF LOST CONFIDENCE

I have a close girlfriend who is beautiful and talented. She is a tall, leggy brunette who is funny and smart. She can sing. She's successful. However, she appears to have no confidence—even though from all outward appearances she seems to have it all. I've even said to her, "I'm not seeing the source of this complete lack of confidence." I look at her and wonder, "Why can't she see how fantastic God created her to be? What's holding her back?" I think most girls are like my friend. There's an epidemic among young women today—the lack of confidence.

An epidemic is described as an infection that spreads rapidly and affects a large number of people in a given population. It's an outbreak of an illness like chickenpox, the flu, or mono that spreads wildly in excess of what is usually expected for a given period of time.

When a girl from my church was in middle school, her class experienced a Hepatitis A outbreak. Unfortunately for her, she caught it. She just happened to be a new student at the school, so no one really knew her yet. She got pegged with the nickname "Hep Girl." Now that's tough: to be the new kid and to be known for catching a disease because someone at a restaurant didn't wash his or her hands before preparing food. Ouch. Years later, this girl told me that she ate many of her sack lunches that semester in one of the bathroom stalls. She got caught up in two epidemics—medical and emotional—and they affected the way she behaved at school.

What's the worst infection or illness you've ever caught?

How did it affect your life?

Just like you experienced the effects of a disease, you'll bear the consequences when your confidence is misplaced or missing. If you "catch" a lack of confidence, you'll end up doing things you never imagined yourself doing. You'll hide out in weird places to avoid the scrutiny of others. You'll do things to get attention. You'll follow the crowd to look cool.

> Then God said, "Let Us make man in Our image, according to Our likeness. They will rule the fish of the sea, the birds of the sky, the animals, all the earth, and the creatures that crawl on the earth." So God created man in His own image; He created him in the image of God; He created them male and female."
> —Genesis 1:26-27

When I was in seventh grade, I was SO flat-chested. One day, I overheard two girls talking about my inability to fill out a bra. (OK, I didn't even really need one yet; I just wore one to fit in.) For days after that, I walked with my arms folded awkwardly in front of my chest. It didn't hide anything. I just looked like an awkward, flat-chested girl.

What's one of the strangest or harshest things you've done because you didn't feel confident?

This is no way to live your life. It's just not what God had in mind when He created you.

THE FIRST WOMAN

Let's take a look at the first woman God created. She doesn't get her actual name until Genesis 3, but we know her as Eve. You can begin reading her story in the first book of the Bible in Genesis 1:26-27. These verses take place on the sixth day of God's creation of the universe.

What do you think it means to be "created in God's image"?

Everything that God had made up to this point was an incredible display of His power, but nothing in His creation so far had the capacity to be in an intimate relationship with Him. Until the creation of humanity, God simply said, "Let there be . . ." and it was. Let there be light. And there was light. Let there be dirt. And there was dirt. He spoke, and it came into being.

But when He got ready to create humanity—you and me, the Bible presents a conversation between God, Jesus, and the Holy Spirit. God said, "Let Us make man in Our image, according to Our likeness" (Gen. 1:26). In essence, God was saying, "I want to be personally involved with this part of the creation. I want to put My hands on them and bring them to life." I don't know about you, but that just does something for me. The Trinity talking about us! I love to picture the Trinity discussing body shapes and hair colors. The way knees and elbows would bend. The way a smile would create crinkle lines around the eyes. The way all of the tiniest neurons and synapses in the brain work together to allow us to function every day.

What part of our physical creation is impressive to you? On the woman provided below, circle three of the labeled areas of her body and describe how God needed to design these so she would have life and beauty and her parts would work together.

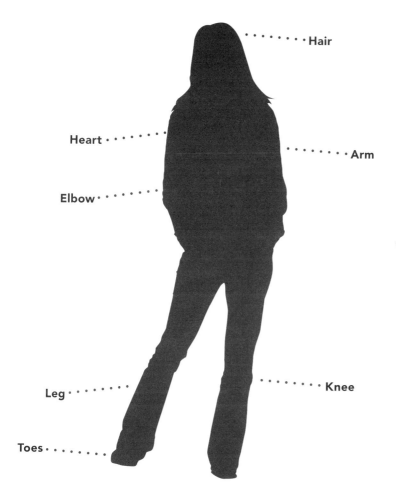

IN HIS IMAGE

More went into our creation than just the way we look and the way
our bodies work. God said He wanted human beings to be created in
His image. We are the only part of creation that bears this privilege
and this distinction. Does that mean God has eyebrows, elbows, and
opposable thumbs? Probably not, since God is Spirit. What makes us
a unique part of His creation is that we share aspects of His character. There are qualities within us that God has too—like courage and
mercy and a capacity to love and to extend grace. Being made in the
image of God allows us to be in relationship with Him. Being made in
the image of God gives us the opportunity to show the world what God
is like by the way we live our lives. Our character and our qualities
help "show off" who God is.

Complete these sentences:

I see the image of God in others when . . .

_____

_____

_____

_____

I see the image of God in me when . . .

_____

_____

_____

_____

Don't miss the end of Genesis 1:27, where the Bible says, "He created
them male and female." That's you, girl. You were God's idea. He made
you in His image. You are sacred and precious to Him because you
bear His image, regardless of whatever standards the world may have.
Because you are created in the image of God, that weaves worth into
the fiber of your being. Your value is automatically built into your
design. You received it as a gift when God gave you life.

VALUE BESTOWED

When Julie was about eight years old, she got a stuffed animal tiger
that she named Tigger. Julie is in her twenties now and still sleeps
with Tigger. He is that precious to her. So much so, that if Julie loves
someone or anticipates missing someone, she asks that person to kiss
Tigger on the nose. (I know it's silly, but hang on.) I am one of the few,
the proud, who have been given this privilege. After all these years,

Tigger actually looks pretty gruesome, but he is one well-loved little tiger. Tigger is of great worth to Julie because she bestowed that value on him. I don't really see it, but she sees it, and that's all that matters to her (and to Tigger).

Describe or draw a picture of your favorite stuffed animal (now or when you were a little girl):

> I chose you before I formed you in the womb; I set you apart before you were born.
> —Jeremiah 1:5a

Why is (or was) this little critter so valuable to you?

You are like that to God. You are of great worth because He chose to impart that value on you—simply because you belong to Him. No one else may be able to see it, but He sees it, and that's all that matters. You can't get more valuable to Him. You don't have to find your value, earn it, or prove it. You are valuable because God said so. He gets to decide what is good. And if He says something is good, then it's good.

I believe Eve was a confident woman. There was no reason for her not to be confident. She didn't have the celebrities and magazines telling her she's not skinny enough or pretty enough. There was nothing to compare herself to that would make her feel self-conscious. —Audra, 15

WOMAN!

In Genesis 2:15-25, further details are given about this good part of God's creation called "woman."

What reason did God give for creating a woman? (See verse 18.)

How did God prompt Adam to understand his need for Eve? (See verses 19-20.)

After God completed each part of His unbelievable creation, He said, "This is good." Only one time did He say, "It is not good" (Gen. 2:18). It had to do with woman's absence from creation and from her place beside man.

God was creative in letting Adam know he needed Eve. God gave Adam the job of naming all the animals. God caused all the animals to walk in front of Adam. As they passed, Adam gave each a name.

At the end of the day spent naming animals, Adam came to a dramatic realization: There was no suitable match for him. No one to share life with. No one to help him work in the beautiful garden God had so generously provided. No one to watch a sunset with. No one to laugh at a giraffe with. So now Adam was ready.

God put Adam into a deep sleep, took a rib from his side, and used it to create "Woman." It's a corny joke, but I like to think "Woman" is called that because when Adam woke up and saw this gorgeous creature standing before him, he said, "Whoa! Man!" Say it fast, and you'll get it. (Told you it was a corny joke.)

What do you think the first woman was like?

Do you think Eve was confident? Why? (Think about your answer. Remember, Eve had no social status, no clothes, and no achievements, and no one but God and Adam knew her.)

_____

_____

_____

_____

_____

_____

_____

_____

_____

_____

_____

_____

_____

_____

I believe Eve was beautiful—inside and out. She had a relationship with God that was different than any other woman to be created after her. Her heart was created with no shame, guilt, self-doubt, or insecurities brewing inside, and she walked with the knowledge that she had a specific purpose in creation. —Jessica, 17

When you look at Eve in Genesis 2, she is a woman of confidence. The Bible doesn't say specifically that she was confident, but she had to be. She was the finishing touch of God's creation, and her everyday life was built on the intimate relationship she had with her Creator.

> "We long for this perfection because the memory of this flawlessness—of being made without blemish in His image—is stamped on our souls. We sense that somewhere, somehow, perfection was possible, but the reality of our sin-marked bodies won't allow us to achieve it."
> —Judith Couchman[3]

Record how Genesis 2:25 describes Adam and Eve's existence:

Describe what you think that was like. How would you feel to be in Eve's situation?

There is no comment on Adam and Eve's height, weight, eye color, or hairstyle. They are described in terms of their nakedness—an indication not only of their lack of clothing, but of their inward condition as well. They were without sin and without shame, with nothing to hide. Innocent. Pure. Talk about a confident woman. Eve was naked, with no embarrassment!

Picture Eve walking with God—naked. Having lunch with Adam—naked. Feeding elephants—naked. What kind of confidence does it take to feed elephants naked? The God-kind. The kind only He can provide. Not the kind of confidence the world gives—confidence based on a new outfit, a good hair day, exceptional grades, an attentive boyfriend, or social status. These are all just temporary. God-confidence is the deep-down-I-can-do-whatever-God-asks-me-to kind of confidence. That's the confidence you were created to have, the kind that gives you full trust in God and His ability to help you live your life as a unique part of His creation.

How would you describe a girl with God-confidence? What does she look like and act like? What is her attitude? What kind of choices does she make? Record your answers to these questions here along with any other thoughts or feelings you may be having:

I believe all of us girls want that "first woman" kind of confidence. Unfortunately, it got lost in the Garden of Eden. Next week, you'll find out why and how it happened. Until then, think about what it means to be that confident young woman. She is part of your original design. I don't know about you, but I can't wait to find her again.

1. "confidence," Dictionary.com, [cited 15 May 2009]. Available from the Internet: *http://dictionary. reference.com/browse/confidence.*

2. "confident," Dictionary.com, [cited 15 May 2009]. Available from the Internet: *http://dictionary. reference.com/browse/confident.*

3. Judith Couchman, *The Woman Behind the Mirror: Finding Inward Satisfaction with Your Outward Appearance*, (Nashville, Tenn.: Broadman and Holman, 1997), 78.

Broken

My freshly decorated Christmas tree fell down . . . twice . . . in one hour. The second time it fell, a bunch of my favorite ornaments shattered on the floor into hundreds of pieces. I said: "I don't even want a Christmas tree this year. It's not worth it!" I ran to my bedroom, slammed the door, and went to bed.

The next morning, beside by my bed sat a box. Inside it lay one of my favorite Christmas ornaments: a hand-blown glass angel. The night before, she was a splintered ornament decorating the floor instead of the tree. During the night, my daughter Julie, knowing this was a special ornament to me, meticulously glued the angel back together. The angel didn't have her original beauty or all of her pieces anymore, but I was glad to have her even if she was a little broken and fragile-looking. Julie did the best she could, but this angel would never be the same unless I took her back to her original maker and asked him to recreate her.

Do you have a broken treasure—something you valued that has somehow been damaged? Describe it and how it was broken:

What would it take to restore this treasure back to its original form?

BEFORE THE BROKENNESS

A brokenness happened to Eve, too, in the Garden of Eden, but to a much greater, more devastating degree. Last week, we looked in Genesis 2 at Eve's peaceful, God-centered existence. We found her naked and unashamed, bringing a beautiful finishing touch to God's creation. Review Genesis 2:15-25 (maybe in a different translation than you used last time), and describe the following as you picture them:

Eve's appearance:

Eve's day-to-day life:

Eve's relationship with Adam:

Eve's relationship with God:

How do you think Eve felt about herself? Do you think she felt valued, capable, and confident? Why or why not? Record your thoughts here:

Being the first woman, Eve had no inherited sin—she was pure and innocent. Think about that for a minute. No jealous thoughts. No mean girl drama. No yelling at her parents. No sibling rivalry. No competition. No lustful thoughts. No worry. No pride. Yet, even though she was created sinless, Eve became the world's first sinner. Something happened to Eve. Genesis 3 tells us the story. Her relationship with God and her God-given confidence are about to be destroyed, and Eve will be broken. You are probably familiar with the story, so go grab a different translation of the Bible than you normally use and read Genesis 3:1-5.

Picture Eve in her newly-created splendor, standing in God's beautiful garden . . . talking to a serpent. I guess everything was so new and perfect to Eve that even a talking snake wasn't a surprise. The serpent basically said to her: "Did God really say, 'You must not eat from any tree in the garden?' Oh, my poor, naive, confused Eve, you don't need

Now the serpent was the most cunning of all the wild animals that the LORD God had made. He said to the woman, "Did God really say, 'You can't eat from any tree in the garden'?" The woman said to the serpent, "We may eat the fruit from the trees in the garden. But about the fruit of the tree in the middle of the garden, God said, 'You must not eat it or touch it, or you will die.'" "No! You will not die," the serpent said to the woman. "In fact, God knows that when you eat it your eyes will be opened and you will be like God, knowing good and evil."
—Genesis 3:1-5

to worry. You won't die if you eat from that tree. God just doesn't want you to because He knows if you do, you'll be like Him—able to see good and evil. He doesn't want anyone else to know as much as Him." The serpent was telling Eve, "Put your trust in something else besides God. In fact, put it in yourself. Then you'll really be something. You don't need God."

Let's do a little comparison by answering the questions below:

Review Genesis 2:16-17, what did God actually say about the trees in the garden?

How is that different from what Eve said in Genesis 3:2-3?

How is that different from what the serpent said in Genesis 3:4-5?

How clear do you think God was about eating from the trees in the garden? Explain.

Why do you believe Eve was tempted by the serpent's words?

_____

_____

_____

_____

God put rules in place to protect Adam and Eve. The boundaries He set were for their own good. God wanted them to trust Him and to experience on a daily basis the life that would come from obeying Him and respecting those rules.

I have a fish in a bowl sitting on my desk. She is safe in her bowl. The borders of her bowl are good boundaries for her. What if my fish could talk like the serpent? She might say, "I don't like this bowl anymore. I want to be like you. I want to have a life of my own on the outside." I could tell her, "You are safe where you are. You don't know what it's like out here. If I take you out, it won't be as cool as you think it would be. In fact, you would die." She (I guess it's a girl!) could insist I take her out of that boundary of her bowl. I could reach in, grab her, and lay her on my desk. How long would she last? It would be painful to watch her gasp for air. Before long, she would miss the boundaries of her bowl. And she would die.

What are some boundaries in your life?

_____

_____

_____

_____

How do these rules protect you?

_____

_____

_____

_____

Which rules are you most tempted to break?

_____

_____

_____

_____

"The serpent made the ability to be like God look perfect—almost like a fairy tale—and I think it momentarily tricked Eve into thinking her actions were OK. I would be tempted by the same thing. As the common phrase goes, 'Knowledge is power.' The idea of consuming something and then instantly having more knowledge is extremely enticing. Even though Eve knew she wasn't supposed to eat the fruit and she wasn't even sure exactly what she would be gaining, I think believing she could do something to be like God led her to do it. She believed she could go against God's wishes and not die from it."—Lauren, age 18

THE BROKENNESS BEGINS

The serpent led Eve to doubt God's Word and then to doubt God's goodness toward her. She bought the lie that her life would be better if she took matters into her own hands and acted like God in her own life. Eve liked what she saw and heard, so she ate fruit from the forbidden tree and gave some to Adam, who ate it, too. By their actions, Adam and Eve declared they didn't need God and wanted to live independently of Him. Like my fish, they wanted out of the bowl. True, they would gain new understanding, but at a terrible price.

Suddenly Adam and Eve were broken. They were forcibly separated from God and their relationship with Him was reduced to fragments, like the shattered pieces of my glass ornament. The rebellion against the authority and will of God had a devastating impact on both. Genesis 3:7-13 reveals how radically Adam and Eve were affected.

Read these verses from Genesis 3 and record Adam and Eve's response to their sin:

Verse 7:

Verses 8-9:

_____

_____

_____

Verses 10-11:

_____

_____

_____

Verses 12-13:

_____

_____

_____

Then the man replied, "The woman You gave to be with me— she gave me some fruit from the tree, and I ate." So the LORD God asked the woman, "What is this you have done?" And the woman said, "It was the serpent. He deceived me, and I ate."
—Genesis 3:12-13

On the mirrors below, compare Eve of Genesis 2 with Eve of Genesis 3. Then record your observations about the dramatic changes in her life. How is the Eve from Genesis 2 different from Eve in Genesis 3?

Genesis 2 Eve

Genesis 3 Eve

But I fear that, as the serpent deceived Eve by his cunning, your minds may be corrupted from a complete and pure devotion to Christ.
—2 Corinthians 11:3

What is the first thing Adam and Eve felt compelled to do after eating the fruit? (See Gen. 3:7-8.)

You're right. They ran for cover. They hid from God.

When Sarah was a little girl, her uncle had a freak encounter with a fly. One night when he was asleep, a fly flew into his ear and landed on his eardrum, causing excruciating pain. (I promise, I'm not making this up. It's not an urban legend!) The emergency room doctor had to squirt water into his ear until the fly drowned and could be pulled out.

Sarah heard her family talking about this, but she was too young to quite know how to process this bizarre news. For years after that, Sarah felt compelled to sleep with something covering her ears. Without that covering, Sarah couldn't relax—she felt unsafe, uncovered, and exposed to any creature that might take an interest in her ears.

Have you noticed that we tend to take cover when we feel unsafe and exposed in our world? Sometimes I'm shocked at the attitudes and actions that spill out of me. For instance, if I think someone is making fun of me, I lash out with my own brand of sarcasm to cover my insecurity. Or if people criticize me (whether it's justified or not), I try to cut them down to size by gossiping about them or pointing out their weaknesses. I find myself asking: Where did that reaction come from? Here's the answer: It came from the Garden of Eden on the day Eve chomped down on a piece of fruit and introduced sin into God's perfect world.

What are some of the behaviors or actions you exhibit when you feel "uncovered"? When you feel unsafe or exposed? When you feel insecure and unsure of yourself?

Adam and Eve's relationship with God was broken, and they were afraid of Him. They had a new awareness of themselves and of each other—including their complete sinfulness before God. They were exposed, not just physically, but spiritually and emotionally as well. They felt the need to cover up. Realizing they were naked, they made clothes out of fig leaves and hid from God.

Where was your favorite place to hide when you were a little girl? Why did you like this hiding place so much?

On the leaves, record some of the places you go or some of the things you do to "hide" from God.

> Be careful that no one takes you captive through philosophy and empty deceit based on human tradition, based on the elemental forces of the world, and not based on Christ.
> —Colossians 2:8

THE BLAME GAME

Adam and Eve felt uncovered, exposed, guilty, and ashamed. They scrambled to cover their sin so they could hide from God's holiness. Through strategically-placed leaves, they attempted to repair their brokenness. Then, to protect themselves, they each blamed someone else for destroying their perfect relationship with God.

Whom did Adam blame? (See Gen. 3:12.)

Whom did Eve blame? (See Gen. 3:13.)

Do you believe the events of Genesis 3 were what God had in mind for Eve when He created her? Explain your answer:

Eve's desires for satisfaction and wisdom were both God-given, and He would have provided a way for her to do both according to His plan. However, she set out to fulfill those desires on her own. What a difference a piece of fruit made. The disobedience of one bite. One sin. And everything was broken. But not just for Eve. It was broken for all women, for all time. When we display these Genesis 3 characteristics of Eve—shame, fear, blame, hiding—we show just how much we are like Eve. Our behavior proves our desperate need for someone to make us new again and to restore the beauty and confidence of our original design.

THE LOSS OF CONFIDENCE

I don't want to put something into Genesis 3 that is not actually there. The Bible doesn't specifically say Eve lost her confidence that day in Eden. However, we can see symptoms of the consequences of her sin, which includes the obvious lack of confidence. It's a reasonable explanation for the different way Eve began to behave. She was afraid and knew that without some intervention, she could no longer be the woman God created her to be.

Every girl since Eve has continued to bear the brunt of this consequence: a lack of God-confidence. Not a lack of confidence in who God is, but a lack of self-confidence based in who we are as daughters of God. I believe most of our emotional, mental, and spiritual issues can be traced back to the day this lack of confidence became a part of our spiritual DNA. It isn't what God intended, but it's a consequence of Eve's sin—and our own sin.

In the list on the next page, check what you believe are the strongest symptoms that demonstrate a lack of confidence. Some we specifically discovered in our study of Eve and still mirror today; some are typical of our

world now based on different circumstances. Review the list a second time and circle the top five symptoms you display in your own life:

- [ ] I'm afraid to try new things.
- [ ] I prefer to blend in and not be noticed.
- [ ] I don't like the way my body looks.
- [ ] I feel territorial about myself or my stuff.
- [ ] I'm defensive.
- [ ] I can't take a compliment.
- [ ] I can't get over things that happened to me in the past.
- [ ] I allow the world to dictate how I feel about myself.
- [ ] I blame others for my mistakes.
- [ ] I'm needy.
- [ ] I don't believe God loves me.
- [ ] I have an eating disorder.
- [ ] I'm promiscuous.
- [ ] I use/abuse alcohol and other drugs.
- [ ] I gossip to make myself feel good.
- [ ] I feel like I'm always competing with other girls.
- [ ] I have to be the center of attention at all times.
- [ ] I lie a lot.
- [ ] I hate myself.
- [ ] I frequently have thoughts of suicide.
- [ ] I assume people won't like me when they meet me.
- [ ] I overspend or over-shop a lot.
- [ ] I make bad choices in my relationships.
- [ ] I believe everyone is out to get me.
- [ ] I am afraid of failure.
- [ ] I feel like I never measure up.
- [ ] I always need to be in charge.
- [ ] I've made too many bad choices.
- [ ] I'm too _____ (fat, stupid, tall, shy, etc.).
- [ ] Other: _____

When we display any of these symptoms, we are displaying Eve's same lack of confidence. This list makes us uncomfortable because we're not crazy about such intense self-examination. But honest evaluations are critical to healing. Otherwise, we stay in our brokenness.

Satan still comes to you and me, tempting us to possess what God has to offer, but not in the way God intends (like sex outside the boundaries of marriage). Satan wants us to give up our confidence in God and make us believe that in order to have the life we want, we have to take matters into our own hands. Not only will self-confidence never take the place of God-confidence, it can also get us into trouble. Eve paid a high price for her choice to find fulfillment outside of God—and we girls are still reaping the consequences of her choice (and our own). We prove it every day with our lack of confidence and the resulting behaviors.

DIFFERENT GENDERS, DIFFERENT CONSEQUENCES

In Genesis 3:16, what two consequences did God place on Eve?

How did Adam's consequences differ from Eve's? (See Gen. 3:17-19.)

Have you ever wondered why the consequences were different for Adam and Eve when they committed the same sin? Shouldn't they pay the same price? Actually, God tailored the consequences to their individuality. Think about it this way: If you have siblings, do your parents discipline you differently?

What sort of discipline works best for you?

What discipline is most effective for your siblings?

After Adam was created, he was first brought into a relationship with God, then to his work, and then to Eve. Next to his relationship with God, Adam would find a sense of fulfillment through work. He would measure his success by his productivity and his ability to carry his share of the load. Work was God's good plan for Adam, and it was assigned to Adam before he sinned.

It wasn't until after Adam sinned that work became difficult. God said: "Adam, your work is going to be harder than it was supposed to be. Nothing will come easily to you anymore." This is why guys gain so much of their confidence from being successful. It feeds into their original design. It's also why they suffer so greatly when the opposite is true—when they are unsuccessful in their work.

Has your dad or a friend's dad or a guy you know ever lost his job? How did it affect him?

On the other hand, after Eve was created, she was brought first into a relationship with God, then alongside her man to help him. Eve would find her greatest fulfillment in her relationship with God and in relationship with others. This is why as girls we gain so much of our confidence through the quality of our relationships. (Unfortunately, that's also why we struggle with issues like gossip and mean girls.)

The consequences of Eve's disobedience affected two of her most significant relationships: wife and mom. God told Eve it would really hurt when she gave birth to her children. (It does.) But most moms understand that this pain doesn't really end when they leave the hospital with the little bundle of joy. Moms continue to be deeply affected by what happens to and with their children. For years, moms have been trying to find the perfection of the garden by raising perfect children.

Have you ever felt the pressure to be "perfect" for your mom? How does this pressure affect you?

God basically told Eve: "You will always struggle with trying to make your guy fulfill desires in you that only God can satisfy. And when he doesn't, you will try to take over and will fight to be in charge." Ever wonder why you care so much about what guys think of you? Ever wonder why it's important for that cute boy to notice your new haircut? Ever wonder why you obsess more over your relationship with guys than you do your relationship with God? Girls are still trying to find the perfection of the garden with Mr. Right, Prince Charming, or whatever we want to call him. We expect all of our relationships to fulfill in us ways only God can. Girls are designed for connection, and if we can't find it, we feel insecure and unconfident.

Name five special relationships in your life. Why are these so important to you?

1. _____

2. _____

3. _____

4. _____

5. _____

If you had to choose between these relationships and being the most successful student in your school, which would you choose? Most of the time, girls choose good relationships. It's how we were created. Go back to the list on page 35. Almost everything on that list connects somehow with the way you feel about yourself in relation to other people. Review the five symptoms you previously circled about yourself. Beside each symptom you circled, describe how this attitude or behavior relates to your interactions with others.

THERE IS HOPE

Let's review for a minute.

Question: What broke Eve's relationship with God and shattered her confidence? Answer: Sin

Question: What could Eve do to put her relationship with God back together? Answer: Nothing.

So what are we supposed to do now? We still live with the consequences of Eve's sin and now we each choose to sin—which means more individual consequences. Will the cycle ever end? Are you feeling as hopeless as Eve did?

You know deep down inside you're not the girl God created you to be. And you're afraid that soon, everyone else will know it, too. There's an ache in your soul that says, "I was meant for more than this." But you are reaching for covering that won't help you achieve the perfection your soul longs for. Your lack of God-confidence leaves you exposed and aware of your brokenness.

As honestly as you can possibly be with yourself and with God, write a prayer expressing what you have felt or are feeling about your brokenness:

Obviously, you need someone to step in and repair this mess and put you back together in your original design. Genesis 3:21 is just a hint of what God wants to do to restore you. It says, "The LORD God made clothing out of skins for Adam and his wife, and He clothed them." We'll study this in-depth next week, but for now, how does God covering Adam and Eve give you an inkling of hope?

Your Creator wants to repair you so you can become all He intended you to be. God-confidence. It can be recovered. You can be made new again.

"I can taste the fruit of Eve.
I'm aware of sickness, death and disease.
The results of her choices were vast.
Eve was the first but she wasn't the last.
If I were honest with myself,
had I been standing at that tree,
My mouth and my hands would
be covered with fruit.
Things I shouldn't know and
things I shouldn't see . . .

She taught us to fear the serpent.
I'm learning to fear myself
and all of the things I am capable
of in my search for acceptance, wisdom,
and wealth."

—Sarah Groves, "Generations," from the CD *Conversations* (Sponge Records, 2000)

New Again

"...just as the Israelites were led out of Egypt by God's mighty hand and outstretched arm, so He has redeemed you and me through His Son's death and resurrection—from our sin and this fallen world and the evil one who holds it in his hands. But even more incredible than what we've been delivered from is what we've been restored to. Because we are new creatures in Christ, the capacity for knowing and enjoying the Creator of the universe, for walking with Him in the kind of intimacy He originally intended for humankind, is fully ours."— Tricia McCary Rhodes[1]

Hide-and-seek. I loved playing it with my kids when they were little. Especially with Josh. He believed if he couldn't see me, I couldn't see him. His favorite hiding place was under the couch. His whole body was hanging out, but with his head stuck beneath it, his eyes were hidden. I'd say, "Where's Josh?" Of course, I could see him, but he didn't know that. Finally, he would peek out from under the couch, and I'd shout, "There he is!"

What favorite games did you play when you were a little girl? Why?

Last week, we learned about a game of hide-and-seek Adam and Eve thought they were playing with God. It began in Genesis 3, when they disobeyed God. Review Genesis 3:1-13.

What rule did Adam and Eve break?

What were the consequences?

Was God really unable to find Adam and Eve? Explain your answer:

COVERED AT A PRICE

Of course, God knew where Adam and Eve were. He just needed them to understand how really lost they were and how desperately they needed to be found—not physically, but spiritually. Adam and Eve needed some action on God's part to repair their broken relationship with Him. But Adam and Eve had to come to that understanding themselves.

What did God do for Adam and Eve in Genesis 3:21? What did that require?

If you were to fashion an outfit from elements in nature, what would you use?

When Adam and Eve sinned, they immediately realized they were naked and felt ashamed because of it. Not only did they become conscious of how exposed they were to each other, they were also aware of how exposed they were before the God against whom they had just sinned. Adam and Eve's attempt to cover themselves with fig leaves was insufficient, so they hid. Then the couple tried to cover themselves up with excuses. God didn't accept any of these cover-up attempts. They were still left exposed and ashamed—physically and spiritually.

God had compassion for Adam and Eve, so He made them clothing from animal skins. He gave Adam and Eve the covering they desperately needed—but He gave it to them at the expense of life. Animals from God's garden had to die so Adam and Eve wouldn't feel exposed in God's holy presence. Their clothing would serve as a reminder of their sin, but also a reminder of God's grace toward them.

The LORD God said, "Since man has become like one of Us, knowing good and evil, he must not reach out, and also take from the tree of life, and eat, and live forever." So the LORD God sent him away from the garden of Eden to work the ground from which he was taken. He drove man out, and east of the garden of Eden He stationed cherubim with a flaming, whirling sword to guard the way to the tree of life. —Genesis 3:22-24

CLOTHING'S SYMBOL

Have you ever thought about what your clothing symbolizes? Next to each piece of clothing named, jot down your thoughts about what each represents:

Sports uniform

Prom dress

Pajamas

Swimsuit

Jeans and a T-shirt

Business suit

Based on Genesis 3, what does clothing actually represent?

Not only did Adam and Eve's clothing cover their shame and display God's grace, it would also be what they needed in the more difficult world into which God was sending them. Read Genesis 3:22-24.

Why did God determine Adam and Eve needed to leave the garden?

How do you think Adam and Eve felt about leaving?

> Therefore, if anyone is in Christ, there is a new creation; old things have passed away, and look, new things have come.
> —2 Corinthians 5:17

Because of God's grace, Adam and Eve were able to enter into a broken world with their God-confidence intact. His demonstration of love by providing the covering showed them that no matter what happened to them, they could trust in God. They could know He was with them and would provide for them in every situation. The key to their confident approach to life outside the garden would be their relationship with God. As long as they relied on Him, they would be secure. Their covering of animal skins would constantly remind them of this.

Just like Adam and Eve, you've sinned. Your relationship with God is broken. Because of His deep love for you, He has provided a covering for you, too. But He didn't cover you with animal skins; He covered you with something much more costly. God brought you back to Him at the expense of His Son's life. The difference between Adam and Eve's covering and your covering is that theirs would eventually wear out as all clothes do. Your covering, however, will last forever. God's covering—forgiveness through a relationship with Jesus Christ— allows you to be new again (2 Cor. 5:17) and to make your way into the world with a confidence only He can grant.

GOD SPEAKS TO US

Let me back up for a minute and explain an important spiritual concept. Through every encounter God has had with people since Adam and Eve, God has used those encounters as opportunities to teach people something about Himself. With Adam and Eve, God demonstrated that He says what He means and means what He says. Sin against Him equals death. He also demonstrated that He has an incredible capacity and willingness to forgive us when we go against Him and His Word.

"All things have been entrusted to Me by My Father. No one knows the Son except the Father, and no one knows the Father except the Son and anyone to whom the Son desires to reveal Him."
—Matthew 11:27

Reflect on significant encounters you've had with God—times when He taught you something really important. What are three things He has taught you about Himself through these encounters?

1.

2.

3.

When God sent Jesus to the earth, He must have really wanted us to learn something about Him and His love for us. Until Jesus came, God had never walked the earth as a human being. In John 14:9, Jesus said, "The one who has seen Me has seen the Father." Jesus came to reveal God to us because in this revelation of God, He knew that we could find real life and be made new again. He not only reflected God ("He is the image of the invisible God," Col. 1:15), but showed you and me how to have a relationship with this amazing God.

ENTRUSTED TO GOD
Read Matthew 11:27.

What has been entrusted to Jesus?

Does this include you? Why or why not?

Review your list of things God has taught you about Himself. How is it that you know these things?

YOU were entrusted by God to His Son, Jesus Christ. Jesus wants you to have the same personal relationship He has with His Father. This is Jesus' assigned mission in your life: to reveal God to you. In doing so, the Son hopes you will be so impressed with His Abba that you will want to be His daughter and become who He created you to be.

MESSAGES FROM GOD TO GIRLS

In coming to earth, Jesus revealed some very specific messages from God to us girls—messages we desperately need to receive and believe if we're going to live a life filled with God-confidence. One of the earliest places in the New Testament you can see Jesus revealing His Father takes place in what's called Jesus' genealogy in Matthew 1. Genealogies are those places in the Bible where there are long lists of people's names—kind of like a family tree.

Starting with yourself on the diagram below, see how far back you can name your ancestors.

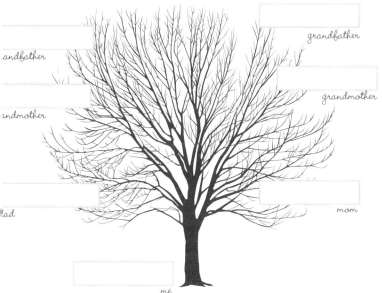

grandfather

andfather

grandmother

undmother

ad

mom

me

Tracing your lineage can be fun, but let's face it: genealogies in the Bible? What's the point? Who cares that Enosh was Kenan's father. Kenan fathered Mahalalel, who fathered Jared, who fathered Enoch, who fathered... (That's in Genesis by the way). I have to admit, I've always thought those were a little boring, and sometimes I wonder why they're even there. But after looking at Jesus' genealogy, I realize those names are recorded for good reason: some of those genealogical records reveal something about God and His desire to restore us to our original design by making us new again.

"There is no Jew or Greek, slave or free, male or female; for you are all one in Christ Jesus."
—Galatians 3:28

God created women as a beautiful, good part of His creation. He intended us to be treated with dignity, value, honor, and respect. By the time Jesus came to earth, however, women were being treated like they were somehow lesser human beings. During Jesus' lifetime, women were treated like a piece of property. Women couldn't just talk to any man they wanted, and they couldn't even touch men who weren't their husbands. Women weren't taught God's Word and had to sit separate from men in the synagogue (church). However, included in Jesus family tree are five women! Listing five women in Jesus' lineage would cause people to look down on Him just because women were named!

Jesus spent His time on earth breaking down walls and destroying stereotypes. He hung out with tax collectors, Gentiles, and women. Jesus taught women, and He spent time with them. He included women in His stories, in His miracles, and in His ministry. He included women as eyewitnesses to some of the most significant events of His life. (Check out Luke 24:1-10 to see who first reported to the disciples that Jesus had risen from the grave!) Every time Jesus had an encounter with a woman, He was challenging social traditions and customs.

What is one of your favorite Bible stories about Jesus and a woman?

Why do you like this story?

In that story, what was Jesus revealing about His view of women?

I love to read the stories of women interacting with Jesus. I think it shows how much He truly cared for them. He loved them no matter what, even if they were hookers." —Anna, age 13

WHY GENEALOGIES MATTER

Focus on Matthew 1:3-6,16. In the margin, circle all of the women mentioned, if you can find them. In just this small portion of Jesus' genealogy are the names of five women: Tamar, Rahab, Ruth, Bathsheba (who is listed in verse 6 as Uriah's wife), and Mary. We're so accustomed to including the names of our mothers and grandmothers that we don't think much about these names being listed in Jesus' family tree. But it's a big deal that these women are included. So what was God revealing by including these women?

God accepts and loves you just as you are. A quick glance at the stories of these women confirms this.

Match each woman with her story:

Tamar	2 Samuel 11:1-5
Rahab	Genesis 38:12-19
Ruth	Joshua 2:1-7
Bathsheba	Luke 1:26-38
Mary	The Book of Ruth (this one's easy!)

These women had bad reputations, unusual marriages, and were involved in sexual scandals. Tamar disguised herself as a prostitute to trick her father-in-law into having sex with her. Rahab made her living as a prostitute. Ruth lived her life as an outsider. Bathsheba had an affair with the leader of the Israelite nation. And Mary got pregnant without a husband.

Talk about having stories you'd rather not tell anyone. I'll bet you have some, too. You have things in your life that you believe will keep God from accepting you. Maybe it's something everybody at your school already knows. Maybe it's secret things you hope no one ever discovers—not even your closest friends.

MY STORY, YOUR STORY

When God found me, I was a mess. I was a total party girl. I didn't care about anything but having a good time. I certainly didn't care about God. The only time He heard from me was when I used His name as a

Judah fathered Perez and Zerah by Tamar, Perez fathered Hezron, Hezron fathered Aram, Aram fathered Aminadab, Aminadab fathered Nahshon, Nahshon fathered Salmon, Salmon fathered Boaz by Rahab, Boaz fathered Obed by Ruth, Obed fathered Jesse, and Jesse fathered King David. Then David fathered Solomon by Uriah's wife . . . and Jacob fathered Joseph the husband of Mary, who gave birth to Jesus who is called the Messiah.
—Matthew 1:3-6, 16

curse word. My idea of a great weekend was to get completely wasted both Friday and Saturday night.

One night I was coming out of my favorite college bar. Standing on the sidewalk, right outside the door, was this tiny, little old lady. As I walked by her, she touched my arm and said, "Jesus loves you." Even with a few drinks in me, the impact of those words was so great it was like she slammed me against the wall.

Not long after that night, a guy I went to college with started talking to me about Jesus. He also said Jesus loved me. I just couldn't imagine Jesus being interested in a girl like me. Didn't He know how broken I was? Why would He want me? I'd never done anything good for Him. I'd wasted my life.

I've been pretty honest with you about my story. Now I want you to be honest with yourself. Journal your story here. Record all the reasons why you think God couldn't possibly accept a girl like you.

Now that you've done that, I want you to write these two sentences across your words: **Jesus accepts me. Jesus loves me.**

Tamar, Rahab, Ruth, Bathsheba, Mary, Carol, and _____ (your name). These are the kinds of girls Jesus accepts. He doesn't care where you've come from, what you've done, where you live, what your social status is, or what other people think of you. He knows you're broken, yet He loves you and knows that He can use someone just like you to bring His hope to the world.

MAKING THINGS NEW AGAIN

God wants to make you new again. Don't you love new stuff? For me, it can be as big as a new house or as small as a new pair of shoes. A new haircut. A new shirt. A new pair of jeans. A new iPod* download. There's just something about "new."

What's something new you have recently acquired?

God is the God of new. In the following verses, underline the word "new":

Look, I am about to do something new; even now it is coming. Do you not see it? —Isaiah 43:19

Then the One seated on the throne said, "Look! I am making everything new." —Revelation 21:5

Therefore if anyone is in Christ, there is a new creation; old things have passed away, and look, new things have come. —2 Corinthians 5:17

Jesus didn't come to make you like new; He came to make you completely new. Not refurbished. Not recycled. Not reused. Not repaired. *New.* New means something has never existed before and now exists for the first time. Second Corinthians 5:17 says that the new you comes from being in a relationship with Christ.

You see, you were created to be in relationship with God (Col. 1:16). But when Adam and Eve sinned, humanity's relationship with God got messed up. Because of your sin, you can't have the relationship either—on your own (Isa. 59:2). However, you can have that relationship you were created for because of what Jesus did for you. He gave His life so He could bring you into a relationship with God (Rom. 5:8; 1 Pet. 3:18). But you have to choose to be in that relationship (John 3:16).

If you confess with your mouth, "Jesus is Lord," and believe in your heart that God raised Him from the dead, you will be saved. With the heart one believes, resulting in righteousness, and with the mouth one confesses, resulting in salvation."
—Romans 10:9-10

Based on Romans 10:9-10, how you can choose to be in a relationship with God and be made new again?

Being in Christ and being made new is a matter of you saying and truly meaning a simple prayer like this one:

Jesus, I know I'm a sinner and have displeased You in many ways. I believe You died for my sin, and only through faith in Your death and resurrection can I be forgiven. I want to turn from my sin and ask You to come into my life as my Savior and Lord. From this day on, I will follow You by living a life that pleases You. Thank you, Jesus, for saving me. Amen.

That guy from college who told me Jesus loved me? He turned out to be Phil, the man I married. He explained the same thing to me that I just explained to you. One night, when I was a freshman in college, I decided I wanted to be new in Christ. I wasn't sure of all the details and my prayer wasn't as well-spoken as the one you just read. But I knew I believed God loved me and wanted to have a relationship with me. I simply said, "God, whatever it is you do, just do it." And He did. He took this wild party girl, cleaned her up, and married her to a guy who wanted to be in student ministry. Me—a minister's wife! No one from my high school would ever believe this one.

God wants to do the same with you. (No, He doesn't necessarily want to marry you off to some guy who's going to be in the ministry.) He wants to offer you a fresh start. He wants to enter into a relationship with you by making you new again.

Do you want to be in this relationship with God? Check the statement that applies to you:

___ I've already been made new in Christ.

Record a brief description of when and how you became a Christian:

_____ Yes! I'm so ready.

Record a prayer, asking God to make you new again through His Son:

_____ Nope. Not interested.

Record why you don't think a relationship with God is what you are looking for:

_____ I just don't know.

Record the names of individuals who could help you discover more about God's love for you. Which one will you talk to this week?

When you commit your life to Jesus Christ, a miracle takes place in your soul. He enters your life, pays the price for your sin, and gives you an eternal relationship with God. You become new, and you know God in a new way. You still look the same on the outside, go to the same school, and live in the same house. The change is not on the outside, it's on the inside. You have a new position in life—God's daughter. You have a new reason for living—God's purposes. You'll start to see things in a new way, hear things in a new way, and interpret life events in a new way.

. . . I have been crucified with Christ; and I no longer live, but Christ lives in me. The life I now live in the flesh, I live by faith in the Son of God, who loved me and gave Himself for me. —Galatians 2:19-20

"Faith is a living, daring confidence in God's grace, so sure and certain that a person would stake his or her life on it a thousand times. This confidence in God's grace and knowledge of it makes people glad and bold and happy in dealing with God and with all His creatures; and this is the work of the Holy Ghost in faith. Hence a person is ready and glad, without compulsion, to do good to everyone, to serve everyone, to suffer everything, in love and praise of God, who has shown him or her this grace." —Martin Luther[2]

Review the two statements you've examined this week:
God accepts me and loves me.

God makes me new again.

What does this do for your confidence?

"When He's on my side, nothing can stop me. When I am thinking about Him and close with Him, I can feel it, and I feel as if there's something in me that makes me different. I am happier and friendlier. I think it's easier to love others when there is Someone who will never stop loving you." —Anna, age 13

No matter what or who you were before, you are new again in Jesus Christ. You get to start over; things are different. You are now in a relationship with the Creator of the universe. You can step out with a different kind of confidence than what the world has to offer. Remember, it's not a my-outfit-is-fantastic, my-boyfriend-is-so-cute, or my-grades-are-exceptional kind of confidence. It's a deep-down, I-can-do-whatever-God-asks-me-to-do kind of confidence. In Philippians 4:13, God, through Paul, revealed the attitude He wants you to have as His new creation: "I am able to do all things through Him who strengthens me."

What thoughts go through your mind when you read Philippians 4:13? Do you believe what it says? Or do you find yourself immediately thinking, "Yeah, but . . ."? Record your thoughts here:

We'll talk more about how to tap into that God-confidence in the next chapter. Until then, remember that you are new again. And this causes God to say what He always says when He creates something new: This is good. This is very, very good.

---

1. Tricia McCary Rhodes, *Sacred Chaos*. (Downers Grove, Ill.: Intervarsity Press, 2008), 87-88.

2. Martin Luther, "confidence," LivingLifeFaithfully.com [online], [cited 18 May 2009]. Available from the Internet: *http://www.livinglifefully.com/confidence.html.*

Everyday Connection

When I first met Emily, she had zero confidence. Every week, we'd get together and discuss what it meant to really live for Jesus Christ. Emily wouldn't look me directly in the eyes and could barely mutter answers to my questions. At the end of our time together, I always wanted us to pray together. But there was no way Emily was going to say one word out loud to God in front of me. I set two goals for Emily:

1. Look at me when you talk to me.
2. Learn to pray out loud.

The first one was actually pretty easy; the second one took some work. At first, I told Emily the exact words to pray, and she repeated them out loud. Then I gave her a general idea of what she could pray, and she would quickly blurt out a short sentence using her own words.

Six months after Emily started meeting with me, she did something that proves God can build confidence in any girl who will daily surrender herself to Him. We were leaving for church camp, and our leader asked someone to pray for a safe trip. Emily jumped out of the crowd, grabbed the bullhorn from his hand, scrambled up on the hood of the bus, and prayed out loud, in her own words, in front of her entire youth group. That is serious progress.

How did Emily get there? She was still the same girl going to the same school, living with the same family, and making the same grades. She didn't look different. She didn't have a new wardrobe or a cute new boyfriend. She hadn't become captain of any team. What changed in Emily? She found out who she was in Christ. She put her confidence in God.

Do you have a "standing on the bus, praying through a bullhorn" kind of story? Describe it here:

If you were to set two goals for yourself—two things you believe God wants you to do, what would they be? They could be as simple as looking at others in the eye or praying out loud. Or they could be bigger in scale, like sitting beside a girl no one talks to.

1.

2.

How will you reach these goals? The same way Emily did. By putting your confidence in God. He created you to do great things for Him, but it's only His power working in you that will enable you to accomplish what He wants you to do. God-confidence means you trust in and depend on the strength of Christ that lives in you.

It looks something like this:

CONFIDENCE CONTINUUM

I can't do anything.
(Unconfident Girl)

I am able to do all things through Him who strengthens me.
—Philippians 4:13
(God-Confident Girl)

I can do anything I put my mind to.
(Self-Confident Girl)

Place an X where you believe you are on this continuum. The goal is, of course, to get you in the middle: God-confident Girl. But if you're like most girls, you have a tendency to swing to opposing ends of that spectrum, depending on how you feel about yourself on any given day.

Let's break it down by reading a description of each girl.

UNCONFIDENT GIRL

"I am Unconfident Girl. I can't do anything. I'm not good at anything. I don't take many risks, because I'll probably fail. I never measure up to other girls around me. There's nothing exceptional about me. I don't believe God has anything big planned for me."

In the empty bubble, record more thoughts Unconfident Girl might have.

How can an unconfident girl's actions and attitudes be a hindrance to God-confidence?

I want to ask Unconfident Girl: If you know that the Creator of the universe has lovingly and wholeheartedly accepted you, then why do you have so little confidence? Why aren't you confident in who God created you to be?

Here's what's weird about Unconfident Girl: she's inside all of us. Every one of us. When interviewed, even the most beautiful super-models express insecurities about themselves. The "it girl" at your school who looks like she always has it together? She's struggling, too. She's just figured out a way to cover up her lack of confidence.

What are three things about yourself that make you feel insecure? What steps do you take to cover this lack of confidence?

1.

2.

3.

The biggest problem about being unconfident is that you're still thinking about yourself too much. Only your focus is on everything you can't do or everything you're not. When you're insecure, you spend a lot of time thinking about yourself and what others are thinking about or saying to you. Anytime your mind is off of God and on yourself, the result is a confidence crisis.

When you fully believe you're significant to God, not because of anything you've done or could do, but because of God's love toward you, then you can't look down on yourself or have these feelings of inferiority. But if you don't bank on the security you have in Christ, you'll search for other people or things to make you feel better about yourself.

Who are people that make you feel more confident? On the lines below, record the names of five individuals whom you want around when you feel insecure. With 1 being the highest, rank them in order of who brings you the most confidence.

What are circumstances or things that make you feel confident? With 1 being the highest, record these below and then rank them in order of which brings you the most confidence.

What is the problem with the people or the things on these lists? Everything this life has to offer you, no matter how good, is temporary and can never compare to the confidence God wants to pour into your life through His Son. Friends change. Circumstances change. God does not. How He feels about you doesn't waver. Ever.

What qualities about God make you feel confident? Record these qualities below and then describe why this makes you feel more God-confident.

No matter how ordinary you think you are, God can do big things through you if you will just surrender your life to Him. You can either live your everyday life overwhelmed by a lack of confidence or you can live with the conviction that when you are not enough, God is enough. Your insecurity does not change who He is.

SELF-CONFIDENT GIRL

"I am Self-Confident Girl. I can do anything I set my mind to. Anything you can do, I can do better. I'm completely confident in my own abilities and don't need your help. Some people may even say I'm arrogant or conceited, but I know that I can take care of myself—on my own."

In the empty bubble, record more thoughts Self-Confident Girl might have.

As a father has compassion on his children, so the Lord has compassion on those who fear Him. For He knows what we are made of, remembering that we are dust.
—Psalm 103:13-14

How can a self-confident girl's actions and attitudes be a hindrance to God-confidence?

Self-Confident Girl may be right. She probably could be just about anything she wants to be. But just like the girl who lacks self-confidence, the overly self-confident girl is focusing on herself. The point she's missing is that she's supposed to be everything God wants her to be. Confidence is not about high self-esteem or healthy self-image based on performance or ability or any outside quality. It's false security; just like insecurity, it's still too much focus on "self." You were not created to look to yourself for confidence. Adam and Eve tried independent confidence in Genesis 3 with horrible results. You were created to find confidence in one relationship: with God through His Son.

What makes you feel confident one day may not the next. Self-confidence is based on impossible and constantly fluctuating human standards. If you try to be confident this way, you'll find yourself running back and forth between "Everybody does this" and "Nobody does that." On the chart below, make a list of things that were in and are now out. Your list could include hairstyles, fashion, music, or favorite hang-outs.

In   Out

By next week, some things on your "In" list may already be "Out." It's hard to keep up. Oh, Self-Confident Girl, you will wear yourself out. In Matthew 11:28, Jesus said, "Come to Me, all of you who are weary and burdened, and I will give you rest." Hebrews 13:8 describes Jesus as "the same yesterday, today, and forever." If you are a girl who leans on her own self-confidence, you need to stop running so hard and rest in the knowledge that Jesus will never move from the "In" column to the "Out" column.

GOD-CONFIDENT GIRL

"I am God-Confident Girl. I'm not afraid to be myself because I know who I am in Christ. My confidence is based on Him. I don't have to find, earn, or prove my value. I just need to live in the value God built into me when He created me. I'm not being a snob; I just know I'm valuable to God no matter what anyone else says or how they treat me."

In the empty bubble, record more thoughts God-Confident Girl might have.

How do her actions and attitudes increase her God-confidence?

I want you to be God-Confident Girl. That kind of confidence doesn't just happen. It takes some work. It means you may have to go against what you naturally feel like doing so you can surrender your life to God's control. Here are four things you can do to frame your life in God-confidence:

So then, my dear friends, just as you have always obeyed, not only in my presence, but now even more in my absence, work out your own salvation with fear and trembling.
—Philippians 2:12

1. GOD-CONFIDENCE: FEAR THE LORD

The first thing you can do to build your life in God-confidence is to fear the Lord. So what does that mean, really? Are you supposed to be afraid to come to Him when you need help? Does that mean He's ready to thump you with a lightning bolt if you mess up? Hopefully, the following Scriptures will clear that up for you.

Match each of the following Bible verses to their correct reference:

_____Proverbs 1:7
_____Proverbs 14:26
_____Proverbs 31:30

1. The fear of the LORD is the beginning of knowledge.
2. Charm is deceptive and beauty is fleeting, but a woman who fears the LORD will be praised.
3. In the fear of the LORD one has strong confidence.

In Genesis 3, Eve became afraid of God and hid from Him. But the kind of fear you just read about in those Scriptures is different from the fear Eve felt. Eve's fear of God caused her to run for cover. She was filled with anxious dread because of her sin. Her kind of fear is what you may feel when your parents send you to your room right before they punish you for something you've done wrong. Or on the way to the principal's office. It's the "my-stomach-is-tied-up-in-knots-because-I-know-something-bad-is-coming" sort of dread.

Describe the last time you felt an "anxious dread" kind of fear:

If you're a Christian, you've been released from that kind of fear. God never wants you to fear Him in that way. It's been replaced with a reverence and honor of God that leads to greater confidence. Fear of God is a hard concept to teach, but here are some simple descriptions of what it means.
Fear of God means:
I honor and respect Him.
I give Him top priority.
I obey Him.
I trust Him.
I respond to Him as One who has authority over me.
I know who He is and live in awe of what He is capable of doing.
I recognize the gap between His holiness and my sinfulness.

Review the list again. Put a check mark beside each statement you believe applies to you.

If you lived your life with this kind of fear, how would your God-confidence increase?

> "I am the vine; you are the branches. The one who remains in Me and I in him produces much fruit, because you can do nothing without Me."
> —John 15:5

I must admit I gain a measure of confidence when I'm successful, or feel like I look good, or other people compliment me. But I try to remember that my confidence should come from finding my identity in Christ, knowing what I stand for, and believing God has a purpose for my life. It should have nothing to do with finding my worth in the world and everything to do with knowing my value to God. —Tyler, age 19

2. GOD-CONFIDENCE: ABIDE IN CHRIST

Abide means "to continue in a place or in a position." Think of all of the places you have lived for a length of time, say at least six months.

List those places (and addresses, if you can) here:

Read John 15:5. What does Jesus say about abiding?

Jesus was telling us that our main job is to stay attached to Him, much like a vine stays attached to the branch. It is through our connectedness to Jesus that His Father can produce the results He desires in our lives, including God-confidence. Simply put, if you spend time with Jesus, confidence happens.

You belong to God. He wants you to produce the finest spiritual fruit possible. He knows what's best for you and gently tends to your

So that they might seek God, and perhaps they might reach out and find Him, though He is not far from each one of us.
—Acts 17:27

heart and life until your God-confidence becomes an everyday way of thinking and living. You begin to blossom with so much confidence that other people can look at you as a "branch" and know to which "vine" you are connected. Your life bears the mark of someone whose confidence is in God.

Two things will help you abide:

1. Deepen the quality of your time with God. Set apart the kind of time with God that builds your relationship with Him. Read His Word. Talk to Him. Worship Him. The more you know God, the more your confidence will increase and the more secure you will become in who you are.

What will you do to deepen the quality of your time with God?

When Christ came, He proclaimed the good news of peace to you who were far away and peace to those who were near. For through Him we both have access by one Spirit to the Father.
—Ephesians 2:17-18

2. Increase the quantity of your time with God. Every day, all day, stay attentive to God. Live your life constantly aware of God's presence, not letting an hour go by in which you haven't thought about Him. In his book, *Just Like Jesus*, Max Lucado calls it becoming "God-intoxicated." If He's going to be the source of your confidence, then it just makes sense for you to tap into that source all day long.

How will you broaden the quantity of your time with God? What are some ways you can increase your awareness of His presence in your life every moment of every day?

3. GOD-CONFIDENCE: APPROACH THE THRONE

There are three people who have keys to my house besides my husband and me: our children—Julie, Jill, and Josh. We gave each of our kids a key to our home with the understanding that they can come in any-time they want. Phil and I are paying the bills and own the house, but our kids have complete access. They don't even have to call ahead and ask permission.

Where is a place to which you have complete access?

Through Jesus Christ you have permission to freely enter God's presence with complete confidence anytime you want. Ephesians 3:11-12 says through Jesus we have, "boldness, access, and confidence through faith in Him." Hebrews 4:16 explains that through Him we can "approach the throne of grace with boldness."

God is absolutely delighted every time you approach Him in prayer and in worship. Every time. He loves when you come to Him, no matter what the situation. Because you are valuable to Him, He has given you a key and complete access. Permission has been granted to you through His Son. You are God's daughter and are welcome to walk right in and speak with Him. At any time. He cares about your life, every aspect of it.

When Jill took Chinese, she always texted me on the way to class if she had an exam: "Pray for me! I'm about to take my Chinese test." I'd text back, "You can do it!" Simple as that. Jill said it gave her confidence to know her mom was praying for her.

Approaching God is as simple as that. You can approach God with your insecurities. There's no time when you should feel like you can't approach Him. I didn't text Jill back saying, "Stop bothering me, you big baby." And neither will God.

Right now, there is probably something you want to approach God about. Express your prayer here using the kinds of words and symbols you might use in a text message.

_____

_____

_____

Look at you. You just stepped right into God's presence. Now, what does that do for your confidence?

_____

_____

_____

What would it do for your confidence if you actively approached God all day long?

This is according to the purpose of the ages, which He made in the Messiah, Jesus our Lord, in whom we have boldness, access, and confidence thorugh faith in Him. —Ephesians 3:11-12

Therefore let us approach the throne of grace with boldness, so that we may receive mercy and find grace to help us at the proper time. —Hebrews 4:16

"God uses ordinary for His glory. He fills a common girl with His uncommon glory. He will use anybody who lays her life at His feet." —Angela Thomas[1]

4. GOD CONFIDENCE: RELY ON GOD

Read Philippians 3:3-8.
In what things could Paul have put his confidence?

Because of his relationship with Jesus, what did Paul consider these things to be?

Think about your life. What are some legitimate things in which you could put your confidence?

What would Paul have to say about everything you've listed?

Paul challenged you and me to have no confidence in the flesh. Absolutely none. What Paul was saying is that things of the world and human accomplishments, which bring you a sense of confidence, are nothing in comparison to knowing Jesus. You can't put confidence in the flesh and in Him at the same time. You can either rely on your own abilities or you can rely on God. Knowing what I know about God, I'd say He's your best bet for real, lasting confidence.

I feel the most confident when I rely on God fully. —Meredith, age 16

So many beautiful Bible verses encourage you to rely on God. It's a consistent theme throughout His Word. Read and underline each of the following in your Bible and then record your thoughts beside the corresponding reference:
Deuteronomy 20:1—

Deuteronomy 31:8—

Proverbs 3:26—

Isaiah 43:2—

Hebrews 13:6—

Choose one of these verses to memorize this week. Write it down on several small pieces of paper. Tape these slips of paper in places where you typically struggle the most with confidence, like on your mirror, in your locker, or on the notebook for your most difficult class.

Which verse did you choose? Why?

Fear. Abide. Approach. Rely. These are all very "active" words. These are attitudes and actions that will bring you into a connection with God and through which He will help you live your life as a confident girl. Now go back to the Confidence Continuum on page 59. Regardless of where you placed your previous X, make a check mark where you believe God wants you to be.

In a prayer, ask God these two questions right now:

❶ God, what do I need to do to make an everyday connection with you?

❷ So that I can live my life as a God-confident girl, what do I need to do differently when it comes to . . .

Fearing you?

Abiding in you?

Approaching you?

Relying on you?

Whatever His answer, remember, you cannot do this alone. But you don't have to. You can be confident in Christ. Now, grab the bullhorn, jump up on the hood of the bus, and be the girl God created you to be!

---

1. Angela Thomas, *Beautiful Offering*, (Nashville, TN: Thomas Nelson, Inc.), 56.

Everyday Battle

Growing up, I went to a small church camp in the summer. Each year, every camper had to participate in a final softball game. I was so bad at this sport that I didn't even have my own glove. I had an aversion then, and still do, to hard things hurtling at great speed toward my face.

So many kids played in this game that the coaches created an outer outfield. There was the regular outfield and then there were additional positions further out. I always volunteered to play right field in the outer outfield. Who could possibly hit a ball that far? I stood counting my blessings, waiting for the opposing team to get three outs so I could trot back to the safety of the dugout—after handing off my borrowed glove to another player.

My final year of camp, it happened. A big college boy smacked a ball up over the heads of the entire infield and regular outfield. This ball was hurtling at great speed . . . toward me. I covered my eyes, stuck out my glove, and missed the only softball in camp history to ever be hit to the outer right field.

I was recently watching a girl's softball game. It was obvious the home team's right fielder shared my same athletic inabilities. But whenever her team headed to the field, she'd ask her coach, "Can I play second base?" He'd politely shake his head and say, "Why don't you stick with right field?" From her position in the outfield, I could hear this girl shouting, "Hey batter, I'm open!" I was praying no ball would be hit to her, but I had to admire the girl's spirit. She was willing to give it her best shot. This girl had some confidence.

Maybe it's not softball, but I'll bet you've had some kind of similar experience. Maybe it's a sport. Perhaps it's speaking in public. Or competing for class president. You had an experience in which:

a. You didn't have the confidence to try; or

b. You had the confidence to do something, even though on the outside, it didn't look like you'd be able to do it.

Choose one of the above and briefly describe the experience here:

You will either live your life like me hiding in the outer outfield or like that girl I watched play softball. You'll either try to blend in, hoping no one notices you and praying you'll never have to take a risk. (And if suddenly you do, you'll cover your eyes and hope for the best.) Or you will live your life asking God to give you a chance to play right smack in the center of the action. And when something comes your way, you'll give it your best shot because you know He values you and has instilled in you a God-confidence that empowers you to take a chance and do something big with your life for Him.

Complete the following statements:
Because I had no confidence, I covered my eyes and hoped for the best when:

_____

_____

Even though no one else believed I could do it, I took a chance and gave it my best shot when:

_____

_____

Whether you believe it or not, you're capable of doing great things for God. Last week, you looked at actions and attitudes that bring you into an everyday connection with God. You learned how fearing Him, abiding in Him, approaching Him, and relying on Him will help you live your life as a God-confident girl.

It sounds so easy when you see it written that way on paper. But putting it into practice in your life is much harder. While you're trying to make those everyday connections with God, you're also fighting everyday battles that will clash with your ability to live your life with His confidence.

Below are a few battles you'll probably face every day of your life. With 1 being the highest and 5 the lowest, rank these in order of how great of a struggle it is for you.

_____ I struggle with valuing the world's evaluation of my life over God's evaluation. I often listen to what the world says about me instead of what God says.

_____ I judge myself by my external characteristics.

_____ Most days, I just don't feel confident.

_____ I'm tempted to find my confidence in the wrong things, such as: _____ (fill in the blank).

_____ I lack confidence because I constantly compare myself to others. Everyone else seems so much more _____ (fill in the blank) than me.

> But the LORD said to Samuel, "Do not look at his appearance or his stature, because I have rejected him. Man does not see what the LORD sees, for man sees what is visible, but the LORD sees the heart."
> —1 Samuel 16:7

Life and death are in the power of the tongue, and those who love it will eat its fruit.
—Proverbs 18:21

So, how can you fight these everyday battles? Here are three ways you can fight back in this struggle to maintain your God-confidence:

1. CAPTIVATE YOUR THOUGHTS

As girls we have a tendency to talk about other people. But how do you talk about yourself? Are you always putting yourself down in your own mind or in front of other people? What do you typically think (or even say) about yourself? The problem with negative self-talk is that you tend to become what you say about yourself. Proverbs 18:21 says, "Life and death are in the power of the tongue . . ." Even the words you speak to yourself have the power to build you up or to tear you down.

Record three negative things you say to or about yourself.

1.

2.

3.

Record three positive things you say to or about yourself.

1.

2.

3.

What does your self-talk indicate about how you feel about yourself?

Does it indicate that you are confident? Explain.

Does it indicate your confidence is based on God? Explain.

One weekend, I hosted a girls' slumber party at my house. At 2 a.m., I thought everything was under control and went to bed. About 3 a.m., I heard girls screaming and running through my house. I threw open my bedroom door and standing there in front of me was a girl covered

in peanut butter and shaving cream. This "goo" was all over my hall-
way. Coming toward her were five other girls covered in peanut butter
and shaving cream. They all froze in place at the sight of me. As they
stood there, the "goo" on them oozed down their faces and bodies. I
said, "What are you doing? This is my house, and you're treating it like
it's a barn!"

We do the same thing with our minds. We throw the door open
and let any thought come in, wreaking havoc on our minds like the
girls who trashed my house. First Corinthians 6:19-20 says, "Do you
not know that your body is a sanctuary of the Holy Spirit who is in
you, whom you have from God? You are not your own . . ." When you
became a Christian, you became a house for the Holy Spirit. He lives
inside of you and cares about what you let in His house. He doesn't
want you to allow negative self-talk in because it has the potential to
destroy your God-confidence.

**What are some thoughts you have allowed in that could be
considered "mind goo"?**

The writer of 2 Corinthians 10:5 wrote about "taking every thought
captive to the obedience of Christ." If you're going to be a God-
confident girl, you'll have to focus on getting your thought life under
control. To put it in simpler terms, it's like making Jesus the bouncer of
your brain.

**Have you ever been to a big concert, restaurant, or a special event
where bouncers were at the door or at the stage? If so, describe what
you saw:**

The job of a bouncer is to decide who gets in and who does not. He
protects those inside or onstage and won't allow anyone in that he
doesn't deem worthy or safe. In the same way, when negative self-talk
or criticism from others tries to get into your mind, you need to cap-
ture the thought, take it to Jesus, and let Him decide if it gets in or not.

For the LORD will
be your confi-
dence and will
keep your foot
from a snare.
—Proverbs 3:26

On the arrows, record negative thoughts you allow in your mind that you need Jesus' help to keep out.

How will taking these thoughts captive protect your God-confidence?

Why will this be an everyday battle?

"One of the greatest struggles I face in finding my confidence in God is that I want everything to work out perfectly. It causes me a lot of stress. When things don't work out, I don't understand why God didn't make it happen."—Amy, age 19

2. SHAKE OFF FAILURE

It takes some serious God-confidence to shake off your past, your failures, and your reputation. Just ask the Samaritan woman. Read her story in John 4:1-30,39-42 and using the outline on the next page, put her interaction with Jesus in chronological order. Before doing that, you need to understand something about the Samaritan people.

At one point in Israelite history, the nation was divided into two kingdoms: Northern and Southern. The Northern Kingdom and its capital city of Samaria were taken captive by the Assyrians. Most of the Jews were sent to Assyria and foreign non-Jews settled in Samaria. A mixed race of people was created when the few remaining Jews in Samaria began to marry these non-Jews. The Jews from the Southern Kingdom thought this mixed race of people were impure and looked down on them. The Samaritans set up an alternative temple worship system based on the one the Jews had in Jerusalem in the Southern Kingdom (although this temple had been destroyed). The Jews hatred was so great for the Samaritans that Jewish people avoided traveling through any Samaritan towns. As a Jew, Jesus had probably seen this prejudice. But He came to demonstrate God's love for all people from every race and nation.

Now, put into chronological order the interaction between Jesus and the Samaritan woman.

_____ a. The Samaritan woman wanted to know why Jesus would even speak to her.

_____ b. Jesus revealed to the Samaritan woman that He was the Messiah.

_____ c. Tired from traveling, Jesus sat down to rest beside a well in a Samaritan town.

_____ d. The Samaritan woman asked Jesus for the "living water" He described.

_____ e. Many of the people believed in Jesus and asked Him to stay a few more days.

_____ f. Jesus instructed the Samaritan woman to go get her husband.

_____ g. The Samaritan woman went back into town and convinced people to come with her to meet Jesus.

_____ h. Jesus offered "living water" to the Samaritan woman.

_____ i. Jesus spoke to the Samaritan woman first, asking her to give Him a drink.

_____ j. Jesus knew the Samaritan woman had been married five times and was presently living with a man.

_____ k. At around noon, a Samaritan woman came to draw water from the well where Jesus sat.

[Answer key: a-4; b-9; c-1; d-6; e-11; f-7; g-10; h-5; i-3; j-8; k-2]

When Jesus first encountered the Samaritan woman, she was purposely alone at the well. Because she was a social outcast, she came to get water when other women wouldn't typically be there. These women all knew her business. They were aware that five men had previously divorced her and that the man she was currently living with wasn't her husband. So to avoid their scrutiny and their gossip, she went to the well at the hottest part of the day.

According to social standards of that time, it's surprising Jesus talked to this woman at all. But that's how He is. He loves to break down barriers that separate people and that make people feel like they aren't good enough. He also knew He was the only One who could

But He said to me, "My grace is sufficient for you, for power is perfected in weakness." Therefore, I will most gladly boast all the more about my weaknesses, so that Christ's power may reside in me.
—2 Corinthians 12:9

bring this girl the satisfaction for which she was so obviously searching. She'd been covering her lack of confidence by looking for love in all the wrong places. And when Jesus questioned her, she immediately threw up more defenses by saying, "I'm a Samaritan. I don't measure up to your standards."

Jesus cut through all of her defenses and changed her life in just one conversation. Wow, what a difference one drink of Living Water made! Suddenly, a social outcast with a shady love life found her God-confidence. So great was her confidence that she headed back to town to talk to the very people who treated her like she wasn't good enough for them. As she ran toward them, I picture her shedding the layers of judgment and criticism these people had laid on her. Yes, she had a painful past with some big failures, but she was no longer going to be defined by those mistakes. Her new confidence was so apparent that the people actually to listened to her and were influenced by her.

If Jesus did this for her, what makes you think He won't do this for you?

Has there ever been a time when you were surprised by your ability to influence others? Describe what happened.

Picture yourself as the Samaritan woman. You have just encountered Jesus personally and powerfully. What would you go back and tell these people?

A girl from a high school Bible study I taught got pregnant about halfway through her senior year. I'd watch her walk into church, and I could just see the weight of what people thought of her pulling her down. She came to me and said, "I can't come to Bible study. The other kids talk about me and look down on me. I don't feel comfortable there anymore." I put my arms around her and said, "I know you've put yourself in a difficult situation, but you don't have to allow them to hang that criticism and judgment on you." She couldn't do it. She couldn't shake off her past, her failure, her reputation. She drifted away, and I never see her anymore.

You can't let this happen to you. Just because someone says or thinks something about you doesn't mean you are forever defined that way. Don't ever forget this: your value and worth come from God. He cared enough to send His Son to die for you so you could be forever defined by His love. It only matters what He thinks of you, and He thinks you are of great worth.

Therefore, we may boldly say: The Lord is my helper; I will not be afraid. What can man do to me?
—Hebrews 13:6

What is a failure from your past that steals your God-confidence?

Write a prayer, asking God to help you shake this off and refuse to let this define you anymore.

Why will "shaking off your past" be an everyday battle for you?

True confidence can be found in God. If you desire an unshakable confidence, you have to lean on an unshakable standard. God knows the depths of my heart and still sees me as beautiful, and that alone builds confidence in my heart. He knows my dirtiest thoughts, sees my sinful behavior, knows my deepest fears and shame, and has nothing but love for me, His daughter. I can't imagine having true confidence without God. —Jessica, age 17

"I am sure of this, that He who started a good work in you will carry it on to completion until the day of Christ Jesus.
—Philippians 1:6

3. PERSEVERE TO THE END

I am a prolific list maker. One of my hang-ups is that when I put something on my list, finish it, and mark it off, I don't ever want to do it again. It's not a very practical outlook on life.

If you were to make a "To Do" list right now, what six things would be on it?

1.

2.

3.

4.

"For it is God who is working in you, enabling you both to will and to act for His good purpose."
—Philippians 2:13

5.

6.

Review your list. Circle those things that could be done quickly. Underline those things that will take time to complete. At the bottom of your list add: "7. Gain God-confidence".

Will this last item be circled because you can get it done quickly, or will it be underlined because it will take time to develop? Explain your answer:

_____

_____

_____

One of the hardest things about being God-confident is realizing that it's not a given—it's not automatic or permanent. It's not something you can gain or master once and for all. Becoming confident is a life-long, ongoing pursuit, a battle you will fight every day of your life. It's a progressive transformation that only God can bring about. But it's something God definitely wants you to have.

MY THOUGHTS, YOUR THOUGHTS

In his Letter to the Philippians, Paul wrote repeatedly about the process of becoming who God intended. After you've read each of the following verses, check it off; then add your thoughts to those I've expressed.

_____ Philippians 1:6

My thoughts: In God's hands, something no good becomes a good
work. God is not done with me yet. He wants to finish
what He started in my life.

Your thoughts:

_____ Philippians 2:13

My thoughts: The work God wants to do in my life is not dependent
on me. It is His work.

Your thoughts:

_____ Philippians 3:12-14

My thoughts: I still haven't become all God wants me to be. But I
want to work toward that goal so I can finish strong.

Your thoughts:

"Not that I have already reached the goal or am already fully mature, but I make every effort to take hold of it because I also have been taken hold of by Christ Jesus. Brothers, I do not consider myself to have taken hold of it. But one thing I do: forgetting what is behind and reaching forward to what is ahead, I pursue as my goal the prize promised by God's heavenly call in Christ Jesus."—Philippians 3:12-14

_____ Philippians 3:16

My thoughts: I want to hold on to the God-confidence He has
developed in me so far.

Your thoughts:

"In any case, we should live up to whatever truth we have attained."
—Philippians 3:16

Why will perseverance in your quest for confidence be an everyday battle for you?

Confidence is a lifelong pursuit of inner strength and determination that can only be inspired by God.

IN ONE PLACE BUT NOT ANOTHER

Learning to live with the confidence that you are loved, valued, and safe in God's plan for your life is something you will work toward on a daily basis. What adds to that challenge is that you may develop confidence in one area of your life, but still lack confidence in another.

In my own life, I'm confident when it comes to working with students, but not so confident with people older than me. And I have more confidence when it comes to speaking to a group than I do when it comes to writing for one. I have fussed over this study with every word I've typed on my computer screen. What about you?

In the columns below, record things in which God has developed your confidence and things that are still in progress. Try to list at least three in each column:

Have God-confidence   Need God-confidence

The goal is to get those things in the second column over to the first. But it takes time. And as you go through your life, you'll find yourself in changing circumstances that will either build up or wipe out confidence.

I used to think I could never go overseas on a mission trip. Recently, God managed to nudge me onto a plane headed for a mission trip to India. First of all, I couldn't imagine myself being able to sit still for a cumulative 22-hour plane ride. Secondly, I'm a hair and make-up girl. I need a shower, a mirror, and electricity for my curling iron. I was there for ten days with no electricity, and I had to bathe every day out of a bucket of water. God and I pulled this one off! Now, I won't hesitate if I have a similar opportunity.

Describe a recent circumstance you found yourself in that built your God-confidence:

_____

_____

_____

_____

_____

_____

Now, describe one that shook your confidence:

_____

_____

_____

_____

_____

_____

_____

See? It's a transformation that takes a lifetime. Don't be discouraged by that. Instead, get control of your thought life by asking Jesus to be the bouncer in your mind, shake off past failures, and run this marathon race toward confidence with perseverance so you can finish strong. Yes, it may be an everyday battle, but you and God can pull off this one!

Daring Confidence

God—He clothes me with strength and makes my way perfect.
—Psalm 18:32

I have a purple dress that only cost me $19.99 from a store way down on the retail food chain. (Let's just say this store would never be found on Rodeo Drive in Beverly Hills!) I have plenty of other outfits that cost more money, but what's funny about this dress is that whenever I have it on, I get more compliments on how I look than in anything else I wear. Whenever I put on the purple dress, I feel beautiful in it. I feel confident because I know it looks good on me.

Is there something you wear that makes you feel more confident because you have it on? Draw or describe it here:

I greatly rejoice in the LORD, I exult in my God; for He has clothed me with the garments of salvation and wrapped me in a robe of righteousness, as a bridegroom wears a turban and as a bride adorns herself with her jewels.
—Isaiah 61:10

WHAT ARE YOU WEARING?

As we've discussed over the last few weeks, real confidence comes from something much more significant than a great outfit. In fact, you've been given something to wear that is like nothing else in your closet.

Read the following verses and record what God has dressed you in:
Psalm 18:32:

Isaiah 61:10:

In addition to being clothed in strength, salvation, and righteousness, Jesus spoke about His followers being dressed in clothes that cover us and indicate our worthiness before Him (Rev. 3:4-5,18). Do you get the picture? Because of your relationship with God through His Son, you've been dressed in the clothing of heaven. I don't know exactly what it looks like, but I do know it looks good on you. When Jesus looks at you, He doesn't see your flaws or your sinfulness; He sees you wearing the covering He provided for you. And He wants you to feel beautifully confident in it.

What does it do for your God-confidence to picture yourself dressed in heaven's wardrobe?

Your confidence must come from Christ alone. It can't be in yourself, in other people, or in whatever the world has to offer you. Your confidence has to be rooted in the assurance that God loves you and values you greatly. Without the confidence that comes from understanding your worth to God, you'll never be able to fully enjoy your life or to become all God created you to be.

AN EXAMPLE OF A CONFIDENT WOMAN

So, what does a God-confident girl look like? How does she think, speak, and act? What choices does she make that indicate her confidence? Luke 7:36-50 contains the story of a woman who gave some answers to those questions. She was daring in what she did for Jesus.

Here is some background on the passage, to help you understand. Women, particularly sinful ones, were not supposed to touch men in public. Both Jesus and the woman took a great risk by having this encounter in a public setting. Because this woman was known as a sinner, the religious man and his dinner guests would have looked down on her.

It is believed that the perfume the woman poured on Jesus' feet was the equivalent to the average person's yearly income. By today's standard, it might be like someone pouring $30,000 worth of perfume on someone's dirty feet. Washing someone's feet and anointing them with fragrant oil were social customs of the day. It would be comparable to offering someone who came to your house something to eat or drink or a place to sit down. The religious man didn't do any of these things for Jesus.

Read the story in your Bible, and then write a quick summary of what happened:

"... they will walk with Me in white, because they are worthy. In the same way, the victor will be dressed in white clothes, and I will never erase his name from the book of life, but will acknowledge his name before My Father and before His angels. I advise you to buy from Me gold refined in the fire so that you may be rich, and white clothes so that you may be dressed and your shameful nakedness not be exposed, and ointment to spread on your eyes so that you may see."
—Revelation 3:4-5,18

What three things in this story really caught your attention?

1.

2.

3.

This woman came to honor Jesus. When she did, Jesus didn't respond to her based on how sinful she was but on how acceptable she was. She was acceptable because of Him. Acceptable outside of everything the world had to offer her. Acceptable in spite of what everyone else thought of her. And the result was a courageous God-confidence. A confidence I hope you'll be challenged to demonstrate in your own life. So what is the result of this kind of confidence?

CONFIDENCE TO SERVE

Being a confident girl is not about some conceited diva syndrome. It is not about demanding that other people treat you as special or as important.

Who is the biggest diva you know?

What has this diva done to deserve this title?

The goal of gaining confidence is not so you can become Miss Popular or Most Likely to Succeed. The purpose of the confidence God wants to instill in you is to give you the courage to serve others. Think about it: Jesus was the Son of God, yet He came to serve. Jesus knew who He was and why He came to the earth, so He wasn't afraid to take the position of a servant. In John 13, Jesus washed His own disciples' feet, a job typically reserved for the lowest of the servants. It takes a lot of confidence to set aside your own wants and wishes and put the needs of others first.

Consider opportunities you have to serve others. For each of the following areas, record an act of service for which you will need God-given confidence:
At home:

At school:

In your neighborhood:

With your circle of friends:

At church:

At work:

Other:

TRUE or FALSE: I have confidence to serve God by serving others.
Explain your answer:

CONFIDENCE TO SURRENDER

In the last chapter, I told you about how I did not want to go to India.
It took a lot of prompting from God for me to surrender to that trip.
About two days after my airplane tickets were purchased, I thought,
"What have I done?" As we prepared to go, I had to constantly remind
myself, "Carol, through Christ, you can do this."

When we first arrived in India, after a 22-hour plane ride and a
near-death experience in a taxi, I realized I wasn't done surrendering. I
was going to have to surrender at every meal and in every bathroom. I
was going to have to surrender to being one of only five English-speak-
ing Americans in an entire city.

I discovered something about daring confidence: **there is an initial
surrender to the overall task God has assigned, and then there are
small steps of surrender throughout the task.** Each moment of surrender requires faith in the reliability and trustworthiness of God.
Each moment of surrender contributes to a new level of God-confidence: I really can do all things through Christ.

It takes confidence to make yourself fully available to Him, whatever the cost, whatever it takes. The sinful woman abandoned her
position in life by kneeling at Jesus' feet. She gave up her possessions
by pouring out her costly perfume. She surrendered her ego by simply
doing what she felt God wanted her to do—whether Jesus and the
watching crowd approved or not.

Is there something to which you believe God has called you to
abandon yourself? Something to which you need to surrender
completely? Describe it here:

You are heaven's Halley's Comet; we have one shot at seeing you shine. You offer a gift to society that no one else brings. If you don't bring it, it won't be brought."
—Max Lucado[1]

What will be your first step of abandonment?

What will you have to surrender at each step along the way?

TRUE OR FALSE: I have the confidence to abandon myself and surrender all of me to God.

Explain your answer:

CONFIDENCE TO BE HUMBLE

Sometimes I'm obsessed with my hair. Should I wear it curly or straight? Do I need to color it or just highlight it? What do others think of my hair? When do I need to get it cut?

How do you feel about your hair?

When did you spend the most time fixing your hair? (as a child, now, for a special event, etc.)

Would you use your hair to clean someone's feet? Explain.

Wait a minute. That last question seems out of place. I personally don't have hair long enough to wipe off someone's feet with, but even if I did, I'm not sure I'd volunteer. Yet, the sinful woman willingly used her hair as a towel for Jesus' feet. We know His feet were still dirty from walking dusty roads because Jesus indicated His host didn't provide any water for cleaning them. The liquid perfume mixed with the dirt must have created quite the gooey mixture.

I had an experience with a pair of filthy feet on a mission trip I took to Mexico. I brought with me a new pair of white women's tennis shoes to give away. I spotted the "lucky winner" of the shoes on the first day. She was a little old lady with no teeth, dressed in an oversized, bright yellow outfit. Perched sideways on her head was a grimy ball cap. But the hat was nothing in comparison to the muck on her feet. They were caked in about a half inch of dried dirt mixed with grass and whatever else she had picked up along the way. I wanted her to have the shoes, but I didn't want to put them on those grubby feet.

I had disposable wipes with me, and I knew what I needed to do. I hesitated, trying to talk myself into "getting 'er done." A local pastor's wife saw my dilemma. Without hesitation, she grabbed the wipes, cleaned up the lady's feet, and slipped her feet into those new shoes. I didn't have the confidence to humble myself that day. The pastor's wife did. Why did I hesitate? I don't want to be that way. I want to have daring confidence to do exciting things for God, but I also want to have the confidence to humble myself to do "dirty work" for God—things that are not exciting but are important anyway.

Why will God-confidence be required for you to humble yourself?

TRUE OR FALSE: I have the confidence to humble myself before God
and before others.

Explain your answer:

CONFIDENCE TO SACRIFICE

The sinful woman poured the financial equivalent of a year's worth of work on Jesus' feet. I don't think the point of the story is for you to spend lots of money on God. The point is that the sacrifices you make for Him should cost you something. The reason personal sacrifice is bold is that you have to believe God will take care of you in the face of what you've given up for Him.

Several years ago, I attended a weekend conference for Christian students. There were probably 10,000 teenagers in the arena. But one girl caught my attention. She made a huge sacrifice to attend this conference. She had been voted Homecoming Queen at her school. This is typically a big deal for girls. It means you're popular. You get a new dress. You get your hair and nails done. The Homecoming King puts a tiara on your head and kisses you in front of the whole school. But she gave it all up because she wanted to attend the conference instead of being crowned.

God took care of this girl. When the event's main speaker heard about her sacrifice, he arranged for a very good-looking guy to escort her out of the crowd and onto the stage. On the podium sat a velvet cape, roses, and a tiara. In front of all of us, she was crowned "home-

> You will be confident, because there is hope.
> —Job 11:18a

coming queen" of the conference. Isn't that cool? She had made a huge sacrifice, and God honored it.

When you sacrifice something for God, He will honor you and bless you for it. You may not be crowned the queen of anything, but rest assured, your sacrifice will not go unnoticed.

Do you really believe God will take care of you if you make sacrifices for Him? Explain.

What is something costly you have sacrificed for God? What was the result of your sacrifice?

> For God has not given us a spirit of fearfulness, but one of power, love, and sound judgment.
> —2 Timothy 1:7

TRUE OR FALSE: I have the confidence to continue to make sacrifices for God.

Explain your answer:

CONFIDENCE TO RISK

Fill in the blank: 2 Timothy 1:7 says, "For God has not given us a spirit of _____, but one of power, love, and sound judgment." Most of the time, it's dangerous to follow God. Maybe not physically, but following Him can be dangerous to your social life. Obeying Him can be hazardous to your reputation. It can cost you friends, a job, or even physical safety.

What are some other risks involved in following God?

God wants you to have an unshakable confidence to take big risks for Him. It was risky for the sinful woman to walk into that house full of men to present her gift to Jesus. She entered a room filled with people who would judge and criticize her. She really didn't even know up front how Jesus would react. He could have turned her away. He could have made an example of her. He could have laughed at her. She demonstrated a remarkable courage to overcome barriers and the perceptions people had about her.

What is the riskiest thing you've ever done for God?

What is the riskiest thing you can imagine doing for God?

TRUE or FALSE: I have the confidence to take risks for God.
Explain your answer:

> My heart is confident, God, my heart is confident. I will sing; I will sing praises.
> —Psalm 57:7

Probably the most daring thing I do for God is trying to talk to people close to me that don't have a relationship with Him. I find the confidence to talk to them by praying about it and by talking to other close Christian friends who give me advice on what to say and how to say it. —Chelsea, age 15

> "I assure you: Wherever this gospel is proclaimed in the whole world, what this woman has done will also be told in memory of her."
> —Matthew 26:13

CONFIDENCE TO SHINE

A similar story is found in Matthew 26.

What did Jesus say about the woman in Matthew 26:13?

Jesus told the people watching the woman that whenever His story was told, the story of this woman would be told in her honor. Although Jesus didn't specifically say this about the sinful woman in Luke 7, it's happening even now. Thousands of years later, when people like you and me read the story in the New Testament, her story lives on as an example. Such recognition wasn't her motivation, but it has become the end result of her act of worship.

After studying the sinful woman, in what ways has she become an example to you?

It takes a lot of confidence to put yourself out there as an example of a godly young woman. You might do great today, and then tomorrow you may fall flat on your face. But it's an inspiring challenge to think that the confident way you live your life today may serve as an example to girls in future generations. Others notice your life and take note. They may never tell you what your example has meant to them, but you make a difference. A confident woman will make a difference.

Describe someone you know who serves as a good example of what it looks like to live a God-confident life:

Name three individuals who look to you as an example of a life lived with God-confidence:

1.

2.

3.

I know a Bible study teacher who always encouraged our students to live up to their potential in God. She wanted them to know that their confidence had to come through Christ and that they couldn't do anything of worth for the kingdom of God without Him. Many times she ended her lesson with this simple phrase, "Shine, baby, shine." With that statement, she was challenging our students to be an example of what a confident Christian teenager really looks like.

Philippians 2:13-15 says, "For it is God who is working in you, enabling you both to will and to act for His good purpose . . . so that you may be blameless and pure, children of God who are faultless in a crooked and perverted generation, among whom you shine like stars in the world." If you take the truths of this study to heart, and if you live in God-confidence, then you'll be as noticeable as stars in the nighttime sky. You'll make people curious about the source of your confidence. A girl like you? With all that confidence? They won't be able to explain it, but they'll want to know all about it. And you can tell them: *It's because of God. I didn't do anything to earn it. I'm this way because of His grace.*

In her book, *Beautiful Offering*, Angela Thomas writes, "I believe when a woman [or a girl] who belongs to Jesus walks into the room, the glory of God should walk in with her. Enough 20-watt-bulb living. Enough private, we-don't-talk-about-our-faith whispering. It's time to be the city and shine! Shine through your ordinary. Shine through your broken places. Just shine!"[2]

On the list below, circle those places where it's easiest for you to be an example. Put a square around places where it's hardest.

At home	At school	At work
On the team	Around guys	With brothers/sisters
With my friends	At church	Online
When I'm texting	At the mall	On the weekends

TRUE OR FALSE: I have the confidence to be an example no matter where I am or whom I'm with.

Explain your answer:

_____

_____

_____

Throughout this chapter, you answered "True" or "False" to six statements. Go back now and add up your answers:
TRUE:_____   FALSE: _____

If you answered mostly "True" to these statements, awesome! You're on your way to becoming a girl who is confident in and through Christ. If you answered mainly false, that's OK. God is not finished with you yet.

As a result of this study, are you different than you were six weeks ago? Explain.

_____

_____

Have you gone from a lack of confidence to a God-confident girl? Explain.

_____

_____

Have you changed from having self-confidence to living with God-confidence? Explain.

MOVING AHEAD

In the weeks ahead as you continue to absorb the truths of this study, you'll be tempted to think that being confident is all about you. It's not about you at all. It's about you being used by God for His purposes. The only lasting, meaningful thing you have in life is Jesus Christ and your relationship with Him. If you can abandon yourself to that, you will go places and do things you never imagined.

Oh girl, there is still so much I want to say, but our time together is finished. I have to be confident that you've received from God what you needed. Can I just finish with a little confidence pep talk?

Your life today is not the end-all and be-all of your existence, so don't live each day constantly comparing yourself to people you may never see again after high school. Don't spend your days existing in the "if onlys" or the "what ifs." To wish you were someone else or somehow different is to waste your unique self—the girl God created you to be.

You are beautiful because you were a brand-new idea fashioned by God and you bear His image. There is only one you, and God wants you to be confident in the individuality He gave to you. You don't have to be anyone but yourself, so you should strive to be the best "you" that you can be.

Know who you are, why you are, and what you're supposed to do with your time on the earth. You are made in the image of God, so act like it! Live loved. Live as your unique self. When you feel that ache in your soul that says, "I was meant for more than this," know that you're right. You were. You are able to do all things through Jesus Christ. Choose to live in that God-given confidence. It looks good on you. Go ahead—shine, baby, shine.

"Our deepest fear is not that we are inadequate. Our deepest fear is that we are powerful beyond measure. It is our light, not our darkness, that frightens us most. We ask ourselves, 'Who am I to be brilliant, gorgeous, talented, and famous?' Actually, who are you not to be? You are a child of God. Your playing small does not serve the world. There is nothing enlightened about shrinking so that people won't feel insecure around you. We were born to make manifest the glory of God that is within us. It's not just in some of us; it's in all of us. And when we let our own light shine, we unconsciously give other people permission to do the same." —*Nelson Mandela in his 1994 inaugural speech*

We come with beautiful secrets.
We come with purposes written on our
hearts and on our souls.
We come to every morning with
possibilities only we can hold.
Add to the beauty.

Beauty comes in strange places, small places
Calling out the best of who we are
To tell a better story, I want to shine the
light that's burning up inside
This is grace, an invitation to be beautiful.
Add to the beauty.

—Sara Groves, "Add to the Beauty" from *Add to the Beauty* (INO Records, 2005)

1. Max Lucado, *Cure for the Common Life* (Nashville, Tenn.: Thomas Nelson Inc., 2008), 33.
2. Angela Thomas, *Beautiful Offering* (Nashville, Tenn.: Thomas Nelson, Inc., 2004), 66.

Leader Guide

Introductory Session

OPEN UP

As girls arrive, direct them to an area where you have provided plenty of food and drinks. If needed, provide name tags. In addition, fill this area with mirrors of all shapes and sizes. On pieces of colorful paper, write: *Are you confident?* Tape these signs in various places and at different angles on the mirrors. For added excitement, play fun music.

Allow girls to relax, settle in, and fill up on snacks. Then give each girl a brown paper lunch sack, five slips of paper, and a pen. Instruct girls to anonymously write five random facts about themselves on the slips of paper and to then put these slips in their bag. Put a large basket in the center of the room and direct girls to put their bags in this container. Then pass the basket around so each girl can take out one bag.

Call on a volunteer to take the slips out of her bag (hopefully, it's not her own—if so, have her switch with another girl) and read each random fact. Lead girls to vote on whose bag they believe it is. Write the name of this "nominee" on the bag.

SAY: If this is actually your bag, take note of whose name has been written on it.

Complete this guessing process until every bag has been assigned to one of your group members. Allow girls to claim their personal bags and to then take turns explaining their random facts.

Promote discussion by asking questions like: Who had the most surprising random fact? Which random fact was the most interesting to you? How similar or different were all of the random facts? Based on these facts, how would you summarize the nature of our group? Are we adventuresome? Funny? Creative?

SPEAK UP

ASK: Who are some famous girls or women who appear to be confident? (You might even want to find and print from the Internet some pictures of famous girls and women who appear to have confidence.) What do you think is the source of their confidence? Who are some girls your age who appear to be really confident? What makes you think they are confident? Do you believe that you are perceived as confident? Why or why not? What is typically the source of a teenage girl's confidence?

Distribute index cards and pens or pencils. Direct girls to define the words *confident* and *confidence*. After several minutes, allow girls to read their definitions. Record their definitions on a small poster board. SAY: These look great. But next week, after we've had time to work through the questions and activities in Week 1 of our

SUPPLIES:
- name tags
- mirrors of various shapes and sizes
- food and drinks for girls
- lively music
- colorful paper
- tape
- brown paper sack (one per girl)
- slips of paper (five per girl)
- pens
- large basket or bin
- index cards
- *Confident* Bible study books (one per girl)
- poster board
- markers
- paper
- pictures of famous confident women and girls (optional)
- journals (optional)
- craft supplies to decorate journals (optional)

workbooks, we may refine these definitions. (Note: Make sure to keep these poster definitions—you will be using them again next week.)

FINISH UP

Distribute the *Confident* books and allow girls to flip through them. Instruct them to write their names in them. Explain that most of the group discussion each week will come from their responses to the questions and activities in this book. Give girls a few moments to read the Introduction. Discuss their preliminary thoughts about this study. Allow girls to share stories similar to the one about jumping from a cliff (p. 6). Talk about the courage and confidence needed to take a leap like that.

Instruct girls to read and complete Chapter One in the coming week and come back next week ready to share. SAY: **This is your workbook. You can highlight things, underline things, and write in the margins.** You might even want to show the girls places where you have already made notations, underlined things, or highlighted portions.

Explain to girls that they will never be forced to share information they aren't comfortable sharing with the group. Remind girls that what is shared in this weekly time together should be kept private and within the confines of this group. SAY: **As we study what it means to be confident, we need to develop confidence in each other. This needs to be a safe place for you to develop confidence.**

ASK: **Are there any additional guidelines we should put in place so you will all be comfortable in this group?** If girls come up with any, instruct them to write these group-determined guidelines in the back of their *Confident* books.

Distribute a sheet on which girls can provide their contact information including name, address, e-mail address, phone numbers, etc. If they are part of a social network like Myspace or Facebook˚, ask girls to indicate this also. Provide girls with your contact information.

Close in prayer, asking God to create a special bond among your group members. Pray that each girl will stay committed to the next six weeks of study. Thank Him for this special opportunity to study His Word together.

In the next week, contact each girl in some way. Let her know you are praying for her and looking forward to seeing her next week. Remind girls of the date, time, and location of your study and what materials they should bring with them each week. Make sure girls know that it's not too late to bring someone new with them to this study.

SOCIAL NETWORKING OPTION

If you have the knowledge, create a new group on the social network (i.e. Facebook) to which the majority of your girls belong. Encourage girls to post discussion questions and words of encouragement as they are studying each chapter. If you're not comfortable with this technology, ask one of the girls in your group to help you set up a site or account for the group. In doing so, you are developing leadership skills in her and building a relationship with her.

JOURNAL OPTION

Provide simple notebooks and craft supplies for girls to create a journal for use during this study. Encourage them to record additional insights, prayer requests, questions, or struggles in this journal and to bring it, along with their *Confident* books and Bibles, each week.

Week One: Original Design

SUPPLIES:
- outfits you like to wear or photos from high school
- two soft drink cans
- poster from the introductory session
- seven pieces of paper, prepared according to the teaching plan
- modeling clay (optional)
- index cards
- pens or pencils

OPEN UP

After the girls arrive, present a quick fashion show of three outfits you like to wear because you think they look good on you. Or show them pictures from when you were in high school of outfits you thought were really cool (or groovy or hot or whatever you called it when you were that age!). Allow girls to make comments. Be prepared for some teasing if you choose to show them this "blast from the past."

ASK: **What outfit in your closet really makes you feel good about yourself? What about this outfit makes you feel so special?** Discuss what a good hair day and a new outfit can do for a girl's self-confidence. Allow girls to talk about a time when a bad hair day or an outfit gone wrong caused a crisis in confidence.

CAN CRUSH

SAY: **It's essential for you to understand the importance of putting your confidence in God instead of people or the things the world has to offer you—like the clothes you wear or a good hair day.** Set out two soft drink cans. Open one and pour out its contents. Show that the other can is still completely sealed. Enlist two volunteers to have a can-crushing contest. Give one girl the empty can and the other girl the still sealed can. See which girl can crush her can with her hands the quickest. (This will take about 10 seconds.)

ASK: **Why did one can crush so easily and the other could not be crushed at all?**

Give this "scientific" explanation: **The open, empty can was crushed so quickly because the external pressure from our volunteer's hand was greater than the internal pressure of the can—it contained nothing but air. The unopened, full can could not be crushed because the internal pressure of the can was greater than the external pressure our volunteer could exert.**

Lead girls to see how their source of confidence is the same way. On page 12, review the list of things that might make a typical teenage girl feel confident.

ASK: **Did you add anything to the list? Which things on this list, in particular, applied to you?**

SAY: **These things people use for their confidence are like the empty pop can. These external things, like good grades or a cute boyfriend, are just not enough to protect your confidence from the pressure of the world. On page 14, you also rated what you believed about a list of statements referring to God's trustworthiness and His love for you.**

ASK: How did you rate?

SAY: Much like the pressurized can, being filled with the love of God and trusting in His abilities gives you something deep down inside your soul that "pushes back" when the world tries to attack your confidence. It is something that fills you from within so that the external pressure doesn't make you cave in.

DEFINITION UPDATE

Bring out the poster from the introductory session on which the girls wrote their group definitions for *confident* and *confidence*.

ASK: Why must God be included in our definitions? Based on what you learned this week, do we need to change our definitions? If so, how? As the girls instruct, make changes to their group definitions. Discuss how including God changed their definitions.

ASK: Do you agree with the writer of this study that a lack of confidence is an "epidemic" among your age group? Why or why not?

ASK: Do you feel like you are a confident girl? If so, on what are you basing your confidence? If not, did your first week of study bring you any hope for becoming confident?

GOD'S CREATION

ASK: If you could ask God one question about creation, what would it be? What is something that amazes you about the human body?

Before the session, using seven pieces of paper, record what God created or did on each day of creation. Distribute the seven papers to seven different girls. Choose a volunteer to take one minute to put the creation event in its correct order by physically moving the other volunteers to where she believes each part of creation belongs. If the first volunteer doesn't get the order correct, continue to call on volunteers until "the creation" is in this order: Day 1: day and night; Day 2: sky; Day 3: dry land, seas, plants; Day 4: sun, moon, and stars; Day 5: birds and fish; Day 6: land, animals, Adam, and Eve; Day 7: God rested.

MODELING CLAY OPTION

Before the session, purchase tubs of modeling clay. Give each girl a glob of the clay and instruct her to form her own likeness. Lead the girls to compare their creations. Discuss how no matter how hard they try, they will not be able to breathe life into their lifeless creations—only God can do that.

ASK: What if I smashed your "dough-self" right now? How would that make you feel? Compare the girls' feelings of ownership to the way God must feel about His creation.

SPEAK UP

ASK the following: **What is the difference between how Adam and Eve were created from the way the rest of creation was made? How have you seen God's image in yourself or in other people? Why is it important for you to understand the care that God took in creating humanity, particularly Eve? What do you think Eve was like? Do you believe Eve was confident? If so, what was the source of her confidence? Do you believe you have or can have the same kind of confidence Eve originally had? Why or why not?**

Direct girls to complete these sentences:

God-confidence is . . .

A girl with God-confidence is. . .

Allow girls time to discuss the difference between self-confidence and God-confidence.

FINISH UP

Give each girl a small stack of index cards. Lead girls to write their names on one of the cards and to pass it one girl to the right. SAY: **During the next week, pray for the girl whose name is on your card. Pray that God will give her a sense of her true worth in His eyes.**

With the remaining cards, challenge girls to record times in the next week when they feel confident. Instruct them to indicate if it was a confidence that came from themselves or if it was a confidence that came from God.

SAY: **At the end of the week, review what you have written. Ask yourself: What do my experiences have to say about my level of confidence? In what or whom is the source of my confidence?**

Close the session in prayer, thanking God for the great care He took in creating each girl in your group. If time allows, pray for each girl by name.

Week Two: Broken

OPEN UP

Before the girls arrive, set out tempting snacks on a focal table in your study area. Beside these snacks, place a sign that says "Do Not Eat." Before the session, enlist one girl who will encourage the others to ignore the sign and eat the snacks. She can lie and say things like, "That sign doesn't include you." "I don't think she means it," or "I don't think anyone will really care."

As girls arrive, hand them each a piece of paper and instruct them to tear it into ten pieces. Set out several rolls of clear tape and direct girls to restore their torn pieces of paper back to perfectly whole pieces of paper.

As they are working to repair their papers, ask: **If the world were perfect, what would it be like? If human beings were perfect, how would we be different than we are today?**

After the girls have worked for a few minutes to restore their papers, discuss how the paper is ruined beyond repair because of what they did to it. ASK: **Is there any way to make this paper brand new again?** Relate this activity to the "brokenness" of Adam and Eve.

SAY: **I told you to tear your paper into pieces. My "Do Not Eat" sign told you not to eat the snacks.** Group the girls into two teams: those who ate the snacks and those who did not.

ASK: **If you didn't eat any of the snacks, what kept you from eating them? If you did eat the snacks, why did you do so, even though it was clear you were not supposed to?**

FISH OPTION

Demonstrate the example from the book on page 29 by setting out a fish in a bowl. Lead the group to choose a name for the fish. Discuss the implications of removing the fish. ASK: **What would happen if I reached into this bowl, grabbed the fish, and laid it on the table beside the bowl?** Make the motion in the water as if you are removing the fish. Your girls will most likely show great concern for the fish.

ASK: **Why is this bowl the safest place for the fish? How does this example apply to Eve? How does it apply to you? What are some "boundaries" in your life? (For example, a set curfew.) How do these boundaries keep you safe? Why did God set boundaries for you?**

SUPPLIES:
- tempting snacks
- sign for snacks
- paper
- clear tape
- fish bowl & fish (optional)
- towel (optional)
- piece of fruit
- pens

FRUIT TOSS

Discuss how God gave very clear instructions to Adam and Eve about which trees they could eat from and those which they could not.

ASK: Why do you think Eve was tempted by what the serpent said to her in Genesis 3:1-5? Based on Genesis 3:7-8, what were the first things Adam and Eve did after they disobeyed God and ate the fruit? Why do you think Adam and Eve felt compelled to cover themselves and hide from God?

Hold up a piece of fruit. SAY: I'm going to toss this piece of fruit to one of you. After you catch it, I want you to complete this statement: Whenever I feel uncovered, exposed, guilty, or ashamed, I . . .

Before tossing the fruit, complete the statement yourself. Then instruct the first girl who caught it to complete the statement and toss the fruit to another girl, and so on, until every girl has had the opportunity to complete the statement. End by asking the last girl to toss the fruit back to you. Purposely miss her throw. SAY: Hey, that was a bad throw. That was your fault.

ASK: Why do we tend to blame others for our mistakes? Is this a sign of a lack of confidence?

SYMPTOMS CHECKLIST

SAY: You spent significant time in your study this week completing a checklist of symptoms that demonstrate a lack of confidence. Review it on page 35.

ASK: Which of the statements describes you the most? Did you add anything to the list? What did you think of this list? Do you agree or disagree that these are symptoms of a lack of confidence? Was this list difficult for you to contemplate? Did you see yourself in this list? What does this list indicate to you about yourself?

SPEAK UP

Discuss the following:

- How did Eve's sin affect her God-confidence? Was God different as a result of Adam and Eve's sin? Explain.
- Why do you believe Adam and Eve suffered different consequences for the same sin?
- What do you think of Eve's consequences?
- Does it seem fair that you still have to suffer the consequences of Eve's sin?
- How important are relationships to you?
- What were some special relationships you listed on page 38?

- What is one of the greatest hurts you've experienced in a relationship? How about the greatest joy?
- Do you agree there is a correlation between the symptoms from the checklist on page 35 and the way you feel about yourself in relation to others? Explain your answer.

FINISH UP

Call on girls to share the prayer they wrote on page 39 about their brokenness. Distribute pens to girls and ask them to turn to this prayer of brokenness in their books. Instruct girls to write Genesis 3:21 over the words of their prayers. ("The LORD God made clothing out of skins for Adam and his wife, and He clothed them.")

SAY: Today, this has felt like a pretty hopeless Bible study. How does this verse give you hope?

Close in prayer, confessing the brokenness of your group, but also thanking God that He provided a way for each girl to be made new again. After the session, be sensitive to girls who may feel remorse or hopelessness about their sinful state before God. Remain after the session to talk with girls who need to be encouraged about the hope they can have through a relationship with Jesus.

Week Three: New Again

SUPPLIES:
- magazines and/or newspapers
- items for make-overs (optional)
- cup
- mirror
- slips of paper
- pens or pencils

OPEN UP

How long has it been since you've played hide-and-seek? Start the session by playing a quick game. Or, if you have time and space, play a game of Sardines. In this hide-and-seek twist, one person ("it") hides and all of the other girls try to find her. Once a girl has found "it" they must both hide together. They may remain where they are or find a new place to hide (without being found by the others!). Each time another girl finds "it," she hides with her as well. The object is for those hidden to remain so and those searching to find the hidden. Use this activity to remind girls of how Adam and Eve hid from God after they sinned.

SAY: **Not only did Adam and Eve hide, but they also created clothing for themselves with fig leaves.**

Instruct girls to look around the room. ASK: **If you suddenly had to make clothing from items in this room, what would you use?**

Distribute magazines and newspapers. Instruct girls to look through these to find various outfits and to describe what they think these represent. ASK: **Based on your study this week, what does our clothing actually represent?**

Direct girls to go through these materials again and look for articles and ads that promote something new.

ASK: **Why do we all love new things?**

Remind girls of the title of this session: *New Again.*

SAY: **By the end of our time together today, you'll have the opportunity to discover something else that can be new: You!**

MAKEOVER OPTION

Provide simple items with which the girls can give each other make-overs. Provide hair products so they can fix each others' hair. Provide simple makeup with disposable applicators. Provide accessories like hair clips and jewelry. Allow the girls to model their makeovers. Discuss how Adam and Eve needed a makeover because of their sin.

SAFE AND SECURE

In both of your hands, hold up a cup (or any other item you choose). SAY: **This cup represents Eve's relationship with God before she sinned.** She was safe and secure in His hands. Place the cup on the floor in the center of the group. Discuss how Eve's sin separated her from her safe relationship with God.

ASK: **Is there any way for this cup to get back into my hands?** Explain that just as it is impossible for the cup to jump back into your

hands, it was impossible for Eve to restore her relationship with God on her own.

ASK: How does this object lesson apply to your life today? Do you believe you are still separate from God or do you believe He has picked you up and restored His relationship with you? Explain.

MIRROR ANGLES

Hold a mirror in your hand and look into it. Angle the mirror until you begin to see different objects in the room reflected. Allow girls to do the same. SAY: This mirror helps us see things from different angles. Describe how God reveals Himself to humanity by allowing us to see Him from different angles. SAY: You can see God in many different places: His Word, in the lives of others, in nature. You can see Him reflected in the lives of Bible characters like Adam and Eve.

ASK: Where are some other places you see God reflected?

SAY: When you see these reflections of God, He is revealing something about Himself to you.

ASK: Why does He do this for you?

On page 46, girls were instructed to record three significant things God has taught them about Himself. Call on girls to share what they recorded in their books. ASK: How does knowing these things about God give you greater confidence?

SPEAK UP

Discuss the following:

- How did you feel when you read about the status of women in Jesus' day?
- Do you ever feel like you are treated differently simply because you are a female?
- Of the five women listed in Jesus' genealogy, who is the most surprising to you? Explain your answer. Spend a few minutes discussing how Jesus came to restore the value and importance of women by the way He interacted with them.
- What do you believe Jesus reveals about God to you?
- Why is it important for you to see and understand what Jesus came to reveal about His Father?
- What do these two statements do for your confidence?
    - —God accepts and loves me just as I am.
    - —God wants to make me new again.

SHARE YOUR STORY

Pick up the cup from the middle of the floor. As you are holding it, share your personal testimony of how you came to understand that God accepted and loved you and that He wanted to make you new again. Be honest with the girls. Express all the reasons you didn't think God could possibly accept you. Explain how God restored your relationship with Him. Describe how you knew you wanted Him to do this for you and how it happened. End by saying, "I was new again!"

FINISH UP

Using the relationship method of sharing the plan of salvation, share the Bible verses on page 51. Explain to girls how God made a way for a restored relationship with Him through the sacrificial death of Christ. Allow girls to discuss the verses and ask questions to make sure they understand what God is offering them (and others).

Lead girls to pages 52-53. Guide them to review the statement they previously checked. **ASK: Does anyone want to change what they previously marked?**

Set the cup back on the floor. **ASK: Would someone like to share how God made her new again? SAY: If you share, please pick up the cup and hold it during your testimony. Then put it back on the floor for someone else to pick up.** You might need to call a few girls prior to the Bible study to ask them to share their testimonies during this time.

End this time of sharing with the cup on the floor. **SAY: If you would like to talk with me further about how to be made new again in your relationship with God, simply write your name on one of the slips of paper I've provided and put it in the cup after we are finished. I will contact you this week.**

Close in prayer, thanking God for your salvation and the salvation of your girls.

Week Four:
Everyday Connection

OPEN UP

Distribute pieces of lined paper and pens. **SAY: Let's pretend it's time for you to make some New Year's resolutions. On your piece of paper, record personal goals you might have for a new year.** Give girls time to work, then call on girls to share three things from their lists.

ASK: Of the goals on your list, which ones will take God-confidence to achieve? Why?

SAY: The main goal of this study is not for you to develop self-confidence and learn a method for achieving your personal goals. The intent is for you to become a God-confident girl who knows who she is in Christ. Today we'll discuss some things that will help that become a reality.

BUBBLE MONOLOGUES

Out of cardboard, create three large "bubbles" like those you see in printed cartoons when a character is speaking. Leave the bubbles empty except for labeling each with one of the following: Unconfident Girl, Self-Confident Girl, and God-Confident Girl.

Group girls into three teams and give each team one of the bubbles and a marker. (If your group is small, then give the bubbles to individual girls or instruct girls to pair up.) Refer girls to the section in their books titled "Confidence Continuum" on page 59. **SAY: Using statements the writer supplied and statements you added, create a monologue that your assigned girl might say.**

Call on a girl from each group to put the bubble beside her face and read the monologue her group prepared. Challenge girls to match their body language, facial expressions, and voices to what they believe their assigned girl might use.

SPEAK UP

Discuss the following by focusing on each girl in the Confidence Continuum:

a. Unconfident Girl:
- Do you agree with the writer that an unconfident girl is still thinking too much about herself? Explain your answer.
- Who are people or what are circumstances that make you feel more confident? How can these be a hindrance to God-confidence?

SUPPLIES:
- lined notebook paper
- pens
- cardboard cut-out bubbles
- markers
- slips of paper
- movie clip (optional)
- DVD player and TV (optional)
- signs (optional)
- inexpensive picture frames (optional)
- craft pens (optional)

- How can an unconfident girl's actions and attitudes be a hindrance to God-confidence?

b. Self-confident Girl:
- What is the greatest difference between self-confidence and God-confidence?
- How can self-confidence be a hindrance to God-confidence?

Refer girls to the items they recorded on their "In" and "Out" lists on page 62 of their books. Call on girls to share some of the items they listed. ASK: **What does this teach you about finding your confidence in people, circumstances, or things the world has to offer?**

c. God-confident Girl:
- Why does God-confidence take work on your part? Why isn't it automatic with your salvation?
- Why is an everyday connection with God essential to the development of your God-confidence?

FEAR THE LORD

Distribute pens and slips of paper. Lead girls to write down things they are afraid of on the slips of paper. Collect the slips. Read each slip aloud. SAY: **If you are afraid of this thing, too, stand up.** Instruct those girls who are standing to sit down after each item is read. If you have time, research on the Internet some different phobias people have (such as *xanthophobia*, the fear of the color yellow!). Read the phobia's name and allow girls to guess the thing feared. You could even make it a contest and award a prize to the person with the most correct answers. (Or award a prize to the most creative answer.)

ASK: **What is the difference between this kind of fear and a fear of God? If you had to explain "fear of God" to someone else, what would you say? How will a fear of God increase your confidence?**

CLIP OPTION

Show a clip from a movie or TV show in which a person is afraid. Be careful to choose material appropriate to the age of your group. You might choose a classic like the scene in the *Wizard of Oz* when Dorothy and her friends approach "the great and terrible Oz." Discuss things the girls are afraid of. See if they can explain the source of their fear. (For example: I'm [Carol] afraid of heights because of an unfortunate incident I had on a Ferris wheel as a 5-year-old.)

ABIDE, APPROACH, RELY

ASK: What do you think of this statement: If you spend time with Jesus, confidence happens. Spend a few minutes discussing this statement, then ask:

- What do you personally do to "abide in Christ"?
- What are some steps you can take to both deepen the quality of your time with God and to increase the quantity of your time with God?
- How will staying connected to Jesus increase your confidence?
- How many times in a day do you typically approach God?
- Do you believe there is a correlation between an every-day, all-day connection with God and your level of confidence? Explain.
- Can you describe a recent experience when you had to fully rely on God? How did this increase your confidence in Him?

FINISH UP

Assign each corner of your Bible study area to one of the following words: Fear, Abide, Approach, Rely. (You may want to hang a sign in each corner to help girls avoid confusion.) Lead each girl to consider which one is her greatest struggle in becoming God-confident. Instruct girls to move to that corresponding corner of the room. Instruct the groups that have formed to discuss how they believe God can help them overcome this struggle. Direct groups to close by spending time praying for each other about this particular struggle. Remind girls that in praying, they are stepping right into God's presence and are approaching the throne of grace.

FRAME YOUR LIFE OPTION

Before the session, purchase an inexpensive picture frame for each girl. Also purchase craft pens the girls can use to write on the frames. Instruct girls to write the following words on the frame, one on each side: Fear. Abide. Approach. Rely.

SAY: I want you to take this frame home and put a picture of yourself in it. Then set it in a prominent place in your room. Whenever you feel that lack of God-confidence creeping up on you, let it serve as a reminder of the confident way in which God wants you to live your life.

Week Five: Everyday Battle

SUPPLIES:
- prepared rectangular strips
- markers
- supplies for relay (optional)
- index cards (two per girl)
- pens or pencils
- cups for each girl
- pitcher or other container of water

OPEN UP

Before the session, prepare the following: Take plain pieces of poster board and cut them into three rectangular strips. On every vertical strip, punch holes in the top corners. Thread a piece of yarn or string through the holes to create a placard. Repeat the process until you have one placard per girl. Provide markers.

As girls arrive, instruct them to use a marker to draw lines dividing their placards into three equal sections. SAY: In the first section, draw a picture of something you personally have wanted to do but have never had the confidence to try. In the middle section, draw a picture of something you had the confidence to do—but from the outside, it didn't appear you should have been able to do it. In the last section, draw a picture of something you believe God has revealed through this study that He wants you to do. When you are finished, hang your placard around your neck so everyone can see it.

Give each girl the opportunity to explain what she has drawn on her placard. Encourage girls to ask each other questions about what is presented.

SAY: It's interesting to see how different we all are. Some of us have a lot of confidence, others have very little. Notice that what is challenging for one girl, isn't for another.

ASK: What does this tell you about developing confidence?

RELAY CHALLENGES OPTION

Create a variety of relays that will challenge girls in different areas: speed and agility, physical strength, artistic abilities, math skills, logic puzzles, biblical questions, and so forth. Group girls into two teams and guide them through the various relays. Take note of times in which girls hesitate to participate in the relay and times when they compete with great confidence. After declaring a winner, discuss with girls how it seems that they each have confidence in certain areas.

SPEAK UP

ASK: What is one of the greatest battles you and God have fought together and won? How did this victory increase your confidence? Why does attaining God-confidence sound simpler than it actually is?

Discuss the everyday battles girls will have to fight in order to be confident.

CAPTIVATE YOUR THOUGHTS

Give each girl two index cards and a pen. SAY: On one card, I want you to anonymously write something negative you say to or about yourself. On the other card, write something positive you say to or about yourself. Instruct girls to put both cards in a container you have provided.

Begin to draw out cards and read what is written. As a card is read, ask girls to determine if it is an example of negative or positive self-talk. Create a pile for each. As a group, determine if their self-talk as a whole is either negative or positive. Then ASK:

- What does our self-talk probably indicate about our groups' level of confidence?
- Why do you believe we are instructed in 2 Corinthians 10:5 to captivate our thoughts and submit them to Jesus?
- What does it mean to take our thoughts captive?
- How will taking these thoughts captive protect your God-confidence? Why will this be an everyday battle?
- What strategies do you and God have to help you get control of your thought life?

SHAKE OFF FAILURE

While discussing the following questions, begin to pour each girl a cup of water. Encourage them to drink it. Then ASK:

- What was your first impression of the Samaritan woman in John 4? How did your impression of her change?
- How does her story relate to your life?
- Why did Jesus call Himself "Living Water"?
- What parallels can you draw between the water in your cup and the spiritual water Jesus wants to pour into your life? How will the water He provides increase your confidence?

Call on girls who are willing to share past failures that continue to rob them of their God-confidence. Share an example from your own life. (Remind group members that things shared during this time together should be kept private.)

ASK: What strategies do you and God have to help you shake off your past failures?

PERSEVERE TO THE END

Lead girls to describe a skill or ability that took a long time to master. ASK: How did it feel when you mastered this skill or ability? Was it worth the perseverance it took to master it? What did this do for your confidence?

Girls may also want to describe a skill or ability they've been trying to learn to do for a long time but still haven't mastered. ASK: **Have you been tempted to quit trying? How much longer are you willing to persevere? What has this done to your confidence? Why is it important for you to understand that becoming God-confident will be a lifelong, ongoing pursuit? Is it worth pursuing even if it's going to be an everyday battle for the rest of your life? Explain. What strategies do you and God have to help you persevere?**

Direct girls to page 81. Discuss their responses to the Bible verses from the Book of Philippians. ASK: **What is the most important thing you learned from studying these verses?**

FINISH UP

Call on girls to complete these two statements:
- **An area in which I have God-confidence is . . .**
- **An area in which I still need God-confidence is . . .**

Lead girls in prayer. SAY: **We're going to go around the circle twice and each pray out loud. (Yes, this takes some confidence!) The first time around, I want you to thank God for a specific victory He has given you in your battle to become a confident young woman. The second time around, I want you to ask God to help you develop confidence in a specific area of your life.** Then close in prayer, thanking God for the confidence that comes through Him.

Week Six: Daring Confidence

OPEN UP

As girls arrive, begin by extending basic hospitality to them. Offer to take their coats or anything they carried in with them. Offer them something to eat or drink. Take your hospitality up a notch by offering shoulder rubs, foot massages, or light manicures. (Make sure it's all done appropriately and in a way that won't make girls feel uncomfortable.) Try to really give girls a feel for your "servanthood." Encourage girls to extend these same courtesies and acts of service to each other.

During this time of serving each other, remind girls of the opening page of Week 6. SAY: **This week, you were directed to read Bible verses about being dressed in clothing God provides.** Then, ask:

- **How does this clothing correlate to the covering God gave Adam and Eve in Genesis 3?**
- **What do you think your "heavenly wardrobe" looks like?**
- **What does it do for your God-confidence to picture yourself in this clothing?**
- **How did it feel to be served today?**

FOOT WASHING OPTION

Call on a previously enlisted girl to sit in a chair you have placed in the middle of the room. As she sits down, bring out a plain towel, a wash basin of some kind, and a pitcher of warm water. Remove her shoes and wash her feet in front of the other girls. As you are performing this foot-washing, give this explanation:

Clean feet were expected when you entered someone's home. When you attended a banquet or a feast, you needed to have clean feet. Generally, a host provided water for foot-washing. Unless you washed your own feet, someone else had to do it. Usually the foot-washer was a person of lower rank—a servant or a slave. It clearly demonstrated who was more important and who was less so. The lowliest of servants washed feet. It was considered such a degrading job that masters couldn't require it of their Jewish slaves.[1]

If time permits, and if you believe your girls are willing to participate, encourage girls to wash each other's feet. If you decide to do this, provide a small hand towel for each group member. If you choose this option, encourage girls to treat this time seriously and reverently.

REVIEW THE STORY

SAY: **This week you studied a woman who performed a humble act of service for Jesus.** Work together as a group to remember

SUPPLIES:
- snacks
- manicure supplies (optional)
- items for foot-washing (optional)
- marker
- poster board
- gift for each girl (optional)

details of the story. Give a volunteer a marker and a poster board and instruct her to record details the group recalls from memory. Enlist another volunteer to read the story from Luke 7:36-50. As the story is being read, have the first volunteer circle corresponding details listed on the poster. Ask girls to call out any additional details that need to be added to the story.

ASK: **What caught your attention when you studied this story? What was surprising to you?**

Discuss the sinful woman's actions toward Jesus. Also discuss the response of the religious man toward Jesus and the woman. Finally, discuss Jesus' response to the religious man and to the woman.

SPEAK UP

Discuss the following evidences of daring confidence:

1. Confidence to serve

ASK: **Why is service the goal of God-confidence? Why does it take confidence to be a servant?**

2. Confidence to surrender

ASK: **What are you currently in the process of surrendering to God? Why does it take confidence to surrender yourself to God?**

3. Confidence to be humble

ASK: **How is humility a direct contradiction to the way the world believes you should be? Why does it take confidence to humble yourself before God? Before others?**

4. Confidence to sacrifice

ASK: **Can you describe a sacrifice you made for God? What did it cost you? What was the result? Why does it take confidence to make sacrifices for God?**

5. Confidence to risk

ASK: **Can you describe a risk you took for God? Why was it risky? What was the result? Why is confidence required to take risks for God?**

6. Confidence to shine

SAY: **Describe someone you know who serves as a good example of what it looks like to live a God-confident life.**

ASK: **How does this person inspire you?**

Refer girls to the Angela Thomas' quote at the top of page 95.

ASK: **What do you think of her quote? Why does it take confidence to "shine" for Jesus Christ? Why is it easier in some places and harder in others?**

FINISH UP

Spend a few moments thanking girls for their faithfulness to this study and to each other. Instruct girls to briefly flip through their books and review some of the questions they've answered and some of the activities they've completed. ASK:

- **What is one of the most important things God has revealed to you through this study?**
- **Do you believe you have become more God-confident through the last six weeks? How will you continue to develop greater confidence?**

To close out the Bible study, pray for each girl by name. Thank God for a specific, unique quality you have seen in each member of your group.

GIFT OPTION

Present each girl with a memento from her time in this study. It could be a candle and candle holder on which you've written "Shine, baby, shine." It could be a journal with a Bible verse from this study written on the cover. Or you could give a compact mirror to each girl and provide craft markers for the girls to use to write the word "Confident" on their mirrors. Whatever you give them, challenge girls to keep this item in a special place to serve as a reminder that God wants them to live their lives with confidence.

---

1. "Foot," "Footwashing;" *Holman Bible Dictionary*, Trent C. Butler, General Editor, (Nashville, Tenn.: Holman Bible Publishers, 1991), 505-507.